CHILDREN'S DRAWINGS

AS DIAGNOSTIC AIDS

DRAWING
François Boucher

CHILDREN'S DRAWINGS AS DIAGNOSTIC AIDS

by

JOSEPH H. DI LEO, M. D.

BRUNNER/MAZEL Publishers • New York

20 19 18 17 16 15 14 13 12 11

"... the soul never thinks without an image."
Aristotle
De Anima

"... drawing consists in externalizing a previously internalized mental image."
J. Piaget and B. Inhelder

Contents

Introduction

In an earlier work, I devoted prime attention to the developmental sequences in drawing behavior. In their striking universality, these sequences attest to the psychobiological unity of mankind. Still resisting the cultural influences that tend to obscure this basic unity, the young child of today, of everywhere, like his proximal and remote ancestor, expresses in drawings the early perceptions of the personal and material environment. Independent observers in many lands have confirmed the identity of the progressions through which the child arrives at the "adult" view of the world—at a visual realism. But while the child is still perceiving naturally, his graphic representations are his very own, quite unlike pictures taken by a camera. Eventually, most children will fall in line and see the world "correctly."

In the present volume, significant deviations from the usual will be explored in greater depth and more extensively than was done in the previous volume, in which but a sampling of the unusual was offered in an effort to show how drawings could be used as diagnostic aids. The reluctance to verbalize often contrasts with the ease with which a child will respond to crayon and paper and unwittingly express what he will not or cannot reveal in words.

The drawings were made in individual sessions under uniform conditions. The order of presentation did not vary. Children of preschool age and those reluctant to separate themselves from their care-takers were observed in the presence of the natural parent, adoptive or foster parent, or nurse. All drawing sequences were elicited by me in person.

Unless otherwise indicated, the children were living with their natural parents.

PART ONE

An Overview

1

REPRESENTATIONAL DRAWING

STARTS WITH CIRCLES

What do preschool children draw?
Does the primitive circle represent only the head?
Quantitative and qualitative characteristics

What do preschool children draw?

As the child approaches age three, his kinesthetic drawings show an increasing tendency to make circular strokes. At first these may be continuous and skeinlike. Soon, they will become discrete circles and, in these, the child will discover that he has represented perhaps, a head. The breakthrough has occurred. Kinesthetic drawing, the joy of recording movement, will gradually give way to the greater satisfaction of creating representational form. Like his prehistoric ancestor, the child has discovered that he can make an image. In the individual, as in the race, the origin of art can be traced to chance.

Universality of the phenomenon has given rise to much speculation as to the significance of the circle as the earliest expression of representational art.

Interpretation seems to vary according to the observer's bias. One might see it as a function of coordination resulting in turn from maturational development of the nervous system, so that the three-year-old is able to do what he could not do earlier.

Another might interpret the phenomenon psychoanalytically, as expressing the child's first perception, his mother's breasts.

The fact is that the circle is the simplest pattern, the universally selected pattern, and the most common form in nature. The child will continue to use it as he represents a variety of perceptions —head, eyes, mouth, trunk, ears, and even hair.

Children who have never seen a woman's breasts, those abandoned or separated at birth from their mothers and reared in institutions, will likewise begin their representational graphic activity with the circle. Might it be a manifestation of the collective unconscious? **(Figures 1, 2, 3)**

FIGURE 1

Spontaneous drawing by a girl of 30 months. She has been living in an institution since birth, has been artificially fed, and has never seen a breast.

FIGURE 2

Transitional. Predominantly kinesthetic with some representational elements. 39-month female, premature breech delivery (birth weight 2 lbs. 2 oz.). Artificially fed since birth. Institution child. Note circles.

FIGURE 3

Spontaneous drawing by a girl of 3 years 9 months. Artificially fed since birth. Placed from institution into foster home at age 1 month. Representational drawing, mostly circles.

Imagination frees the spirit from
the bonds of reality

The child, in his early attempts at representation, does not try to draw the object as it looks but the idea, the internal model, and produces a schematic reduction to essentials. Luquet termed this *intellectual realism* to distinguish it from the *visual realism* of the adult. Great artists of our time, notably Klee, have sought to recapture the memory images of childhood and the child's capacity to picture some of what he knows.

Piaget observed that the transition from intellectual realism to visual realism is not limited to drawing but characterizes all of the child's mental processes—the young child's reality is of his own mental construction, and the child's vision is distorted by his ideas.

C. Ricci (Italy), writing in 1885, noted how young children drew what they knew existed and not what was actually seen, and illustrated the principle with fascinating reproductions of drawings showing men visible through the hulls of ships, men on horseback astride but showing both legs, and a bell-ringer inside the bell-tower. What exists must be shown.

In analyzing the first stage in development of the figurative arts, I. Piotrowska (Poland) tells how children draw the known and not the seen reality, and how the figures are exaggerated by affective and expressive influences.

H. Eng (Norway) studied the drawings of her niece from the earliest scribblings to age eight. Her observations confirmed those of investigators in other countries—that the child's first recognizable drawing is usually a human figure, and that the child draws what he knows and not what is seen.

The child's drawing of a person is identical whether a person or other model is before him or whether he draws from memory.

M. Prudhommeau (France) states that the child does not draw the object as it is but draws his idea of it, that is, his *modèle interne*.

W. Wolff (U.S.A.), noting that children's art refers to an inner realism, added an important dimension to our understanding by indicating that a most important element, the emotional factor, influences the child's concept and drawings.

H. G. Spearing (England) found that children do not try to

draw what they can actually see, but what they remember; and that it is only later that they will be influenced by what is actually seen and by suggestion, instruction, and direction.

H. Read agreed that what is drawn is a mental impression rather than a visual observation. He, too, noted that the representation is not purely intellectual but imbued with emotional elements.

On pages 103 and 104 of my book *Young Children and Their Drawings*, the reader may see an amusing example of "drawing what is known to exist." A preschool boy, having drawn what he called a cow, turned the paper over to draw the tail behind, much like Spearing's description of the little girl who, on being given a picture of a bird in profile, asked why it had only one eye, then "not satisfied with the explanation, she turned the paper over and drew the other eye."

I have offered some representative opinions in support of the important principle that drawings by young children are representations and not reproduction, that they express an inner and not a visual realism. The drawings make a statement about the child himself and less about the object drawn. The image is imbued with affective as well as cognitive elements.

Yet R. Arnheim claims that the child draws what he sees. It seems to me that this contrastingly expressed view is only in semantic conflict with that of the others mentioned. The conflict revolves about the word "sees." If I am interpreting him correctly, Arnheim does not use the word "see" to indicate a mere *sensation*. He does not equate the retinal image with the one recorded through the lens of a camera. He holds that the eye has already made a selection of the many visual stimuli that compose an image. This selection is already a mental process and is an aspect of visual thinking. What we see, what the young child sees is not what the inert, non-living camera sees. May I add that it is for the same reason that two persons looking at the same object do not see it in the same way. An amusing cartoon in a magazine shows an elderly couple walking. Coming in the opposite direction is an attractive, generously-endowed girl. Above the husband and wife is a vision of what each of them sees as she approaches. The wife sees a dress, the husband a girl—no dress.

What we see—and this applies as well to the child—is influenced by what we have seen, what we remember at that moment, and by how we feel and think about it.

In summary, observers past and present, here and abroad,

have given the following answers to the question "What do children draw?":

1. what is important to them: predominantly people, then animals, houses, trees;
2. some, but not all of what is known about the object;
3. what is remembered at the time;
4. the idea colored by feelings;
5. what is seen (in the sense used by Arnheim);
6. an inner, not an optical reality.

Hence, children are expressionists for whom the object serves merely as a cue or catalyst. Whether drawing from a model or from memory, the result is the same.

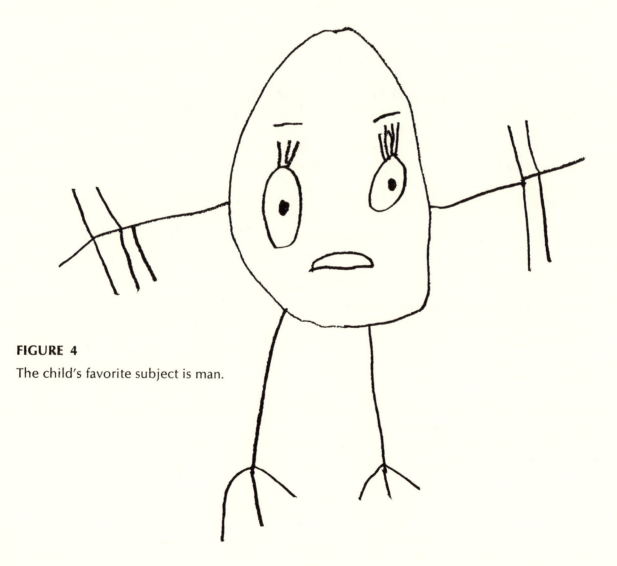

FIGURE 4

The child's favorite subject is man.

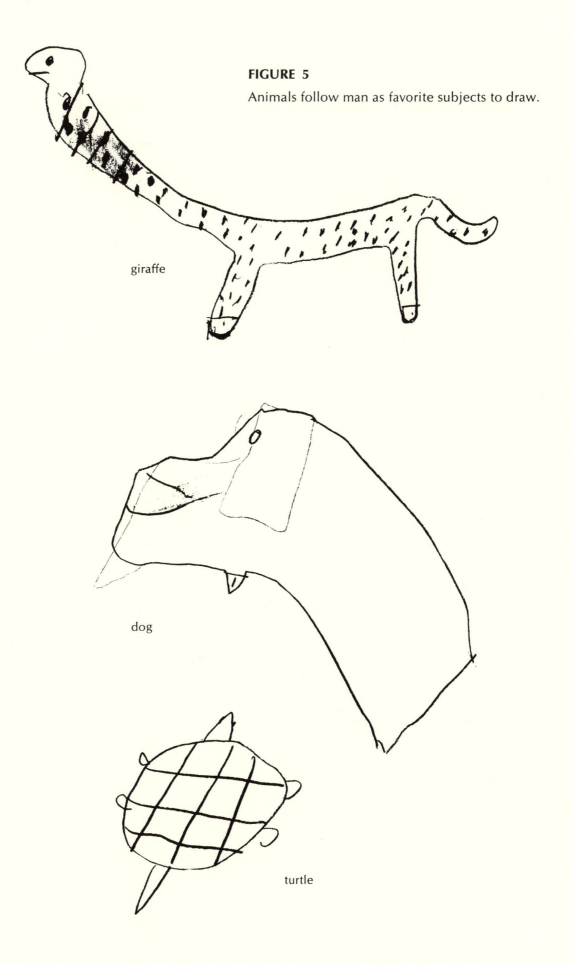

FIGURE 5

Animals follow man as favorite subjects to draw.

giraffe

dog

turtle

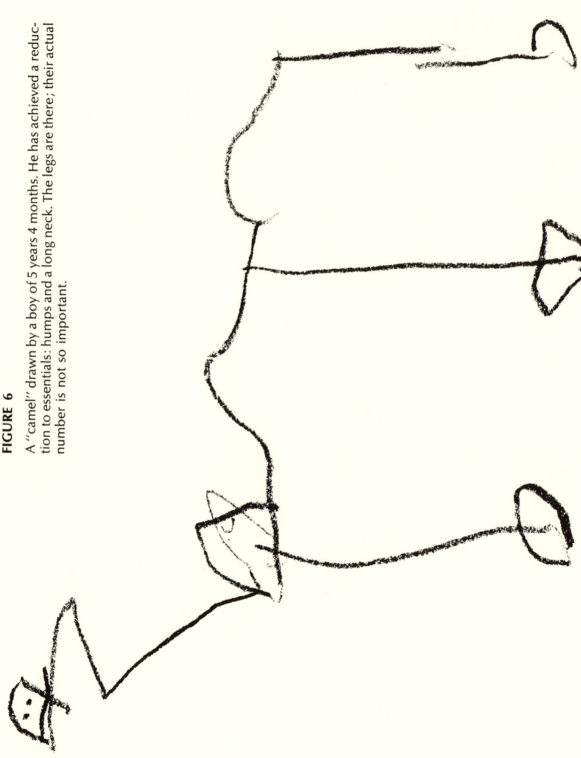

FIGURE 6

A "camel" drawn by a boy of 5 years 4 months. He has achieved a reduction to essentials: humps and a long neck. The legs are there; their actual number is not so important.

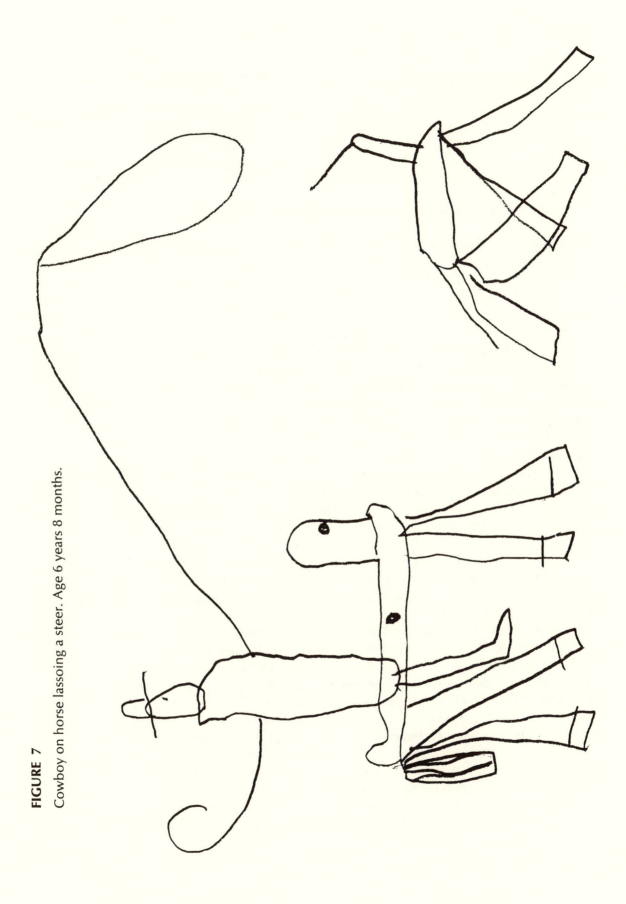

FIGURE 7
Cowboy on horse lassoing a steer. Age 6 years 8 months.

Does the primitive circle represent only the head?

What may seem to be a futile question has a basic significance insofar as it relates to interpretation of the earliest human figure drawings. The generally held view is that the child represents a person by what is most essential. Even as an infant, nothing was as interesting as a face. Fascinated by the circular configuration wherein resides what eats, talks, sees, hears, smiles, and frowns, little wonder that the child should select that part of the anatomy as representing the person. The next step will be to provide it with the appendages that move it from place to place. Hence, the comical figure produced by children of four and five, today and yesterday, here and abroad. Quite fittingly, it is called tadpole, cephalopod, *Kopffüssler, bonhomme tétard*, all terms descriptive of the little person, all head and legs, so unreal and yet so unmistakably human —an uncanny reduction to essentials.

But there are dissenting voices: Britsch, Mühle, and especially Arnheim, who in a discussion titled "The Misnamed Tadpoles" takes issue with the generally espoused view, calling it "the most striking case of misinterpretation due to realistic bias." He claims that the trunk is not left out, that the trunk is included within the circle, and that consequently the limbs are correctly attached and that the term "tadpole" is erroneously applied and misleading (R. Arnheim, *Art and Visual Perception*, p. 188).

Later, when after age five children begin to draw a second circle to represent the body, the primacy of the head is proclaimed by its exaggerated size. Arnheim disagrees with those of us who believe that the head is drawn large because it is the most important part and symbolic of the person. He attributes the exaggeration to mere lack of space in which to draw the rest of the figure once the child has drawn a large circle in the center of the page.

On this issue I must disagree with Arnheim, having seen innumerable drawings in which the circle and features clearly represent the head and nothing more. **Figure 9,** drawn by a girl of 38 months, is a representative example. As she drew, she named the parts in the following order: legs, face, eyes, arms. On finishing the

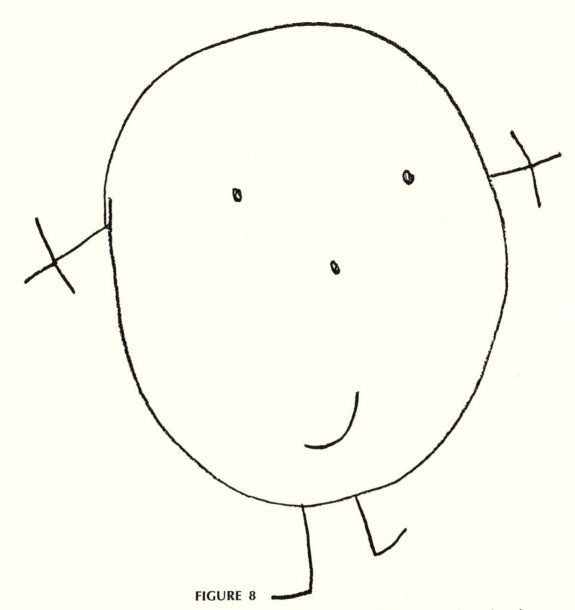

Primacy of the head. Human figure drawn by a female foster child of 4 years 11 months. Average intelligence. There is no trunk. She said to the examiner, "a big head."

drawing, she handed it to me and said "it's mommie." Apart from the fact that she is a bright child whose drawing expresses a 4-year-old concept of body image, one cannot but be impressed by the clear designation of the circle as a "face" into which she has drawn the "eyes."

Figure 10, drawn by a child of 4 years 10 months, clearly shows that omission of the trunk is not due to lack of space; nor is the head so disproportionately large because the rest could not be squeezed into the remaining space.

FIGURE 9

Human figure drawn by a girl of 3 years 2 months. She pointed to the circle and said "her face." This statement clearly indicates that the circle does not include the trunk.

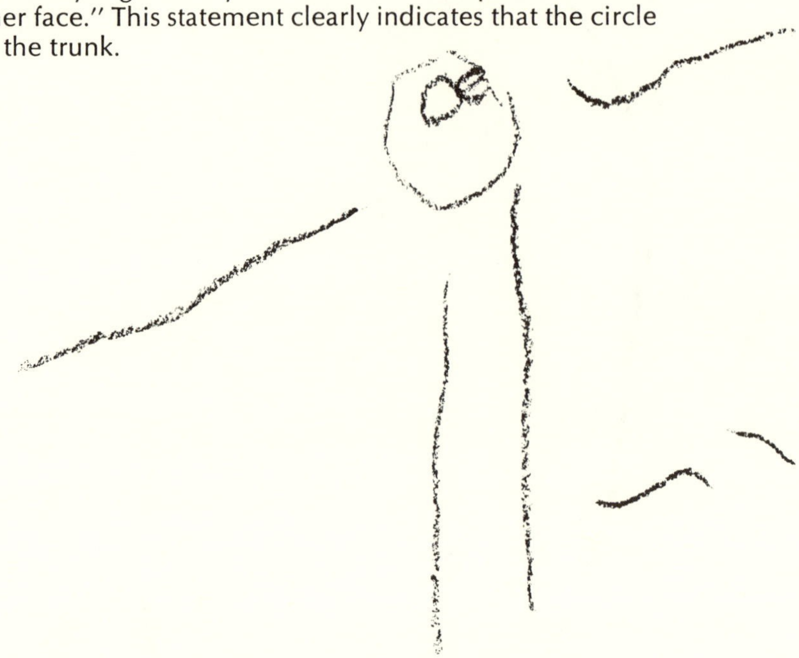

FIGURE 10

Human figure by a bright girl of 4 years 10 months. Absence of the trunk is obviously not due to lack of space.

FIGURE 11

Drawn by a girl aged 5 years 7 months. Absence of trunk is clearly not due to lack of space.

FIGURE 12

Drawn by a bright Chinese girl of 5 years 3 months.

Quantitative and qualitative characteristics

Quantitative differences in drawings of the human figure have been related to chronological age and intellectual maturity, forming the basis for assessment of intelligence. But while there is general agreement that qualitative differences can be identified in the drawings, there is much diversity of opinion as to the meaning of the differences. A voluminous literature dealing with the subject attests to the importance with which the problem is viewed by psychologists, psychiatrists, pediatricians, educators, and artists. It seems fair to say that we all know there is something revealing of the child himself, something intimately personal that will help to understand the child and his problem. Apart from specific features, there are general, overall impressions that are designated by terms such as "grotesque, bizarre, distorted, disorganized, constricted, vague, inhibited, weak" or by their opposites, "realistic, pleasant, well-proportioned, integrated, expansive, well-defined, uninhibited, bold."

The validity of human figure drawings as expressions of intellectual maturity has been established. Can the same be said for the drawings as expressions of personality? Are there specific items or general characteristics that can be related to behavioral syndromes? If so, might they not form the basis for an evaluative scale?

A review of the literature shows that numerous attempts have been made to do that very thing, to introduce scientific objectivity into what continues to be a highly subjective, clinical procedure. K. Machover has been especially interested in this problem and has made valuable contributions to our interpretation of the drawings.

Even at the cost of irritating the reader, I must emphasize what I consider a basic premise to any valid interpretation. *Knowledge of developmental sequences is essential lest one consider deviant what is merely the immaturity of a normally developing psyche.*

2

THE BODY IMAGE

Is the child's human figure drawing a self-image?
Black and white
Body image and perception

"The experience of one's own body is the basis for all other life experiences."
Paul Schilder

Is the child's human figure drawing a self-image?

The child's maturing concept of the body image is reflected in increasing complexity of his human figure drawing. The sequences are strikingly similar in children widely separated in time and space, a fact that proclaims the basic unity of mankind and, more precisely, a biological kinship that extends into the less tangible realities of mentation and emotions.

Central to one's concept of the body image is the awareness of one's own body. Perception of Self is the base from which sensations from the environment become meaningful. During the second half of the first year, the infant gradually becomes aware of the separation that exists between Self and the environment, that the mother-child dyad is not a oneness. There will be a gradual attainment of a sense of individuality as the infant becomes aware of parts of the body, of their position in space, and of his ability to control their movements, and eventually to respond appropriately to tactile, visual, auditory, and other sensations from the Outside.

For a time, I too subscribed to the widely accepted view that the child's drawing was a self-image. I have since learned to question this assertion, despite unequivocal statements by numerous authorities to that effect. While it is a fact that the vast majority of children will draw a person of their own sex, it is also true that the human figure they draw spontaneously is an adult and not a child. The child seems to be more interested in grown-ups than in himself. It is only later, when old enough to draw his family, that he will point to one of the figures and say "that's me" besides including his siblings. There are instances in which the child unmistakably draws a self-image, as when a child, beset by fears and anxieties, drew a weeping child.

As I have watched children draw over many years and have studied their products, I have come to believe that when a child is well adjusted and free from anxiety, his intellect is free, behavior is exteriorized. In responding to the environment, the child, fascinated by the Outside, forgets himself and expresses in drawing a concept of humankind rather than just of the Self. The Self is included and absorbed.

A similar situation prevails on the physical plane. We are not aware of heart or stomach unless they are hurting or bothering. Ordinarily we are completely taken up with business or pleasure as the case may be. The more well adjusted we are the less are we inclined to worry or even think about ourselves. The child who is not tormented by anxiety forgets the Self in a thorough involvement with the world of persons and things. And when he draws a person, the result is more likely to be a schema that represents the significant adult in his world.

If this interpretation is correct, as I believe it to be, it adds validity to the diagnostic use of drawings by children who have emotional problems. Their drawings will tend to be imbued with symbolic elements expressive of their disorder.

Drawings by well adjusted children are strikingly similar. Those by the emotionally disturbed are strikingly different from those and from each other, as each child is disturbed in his own special way.

In studying the drawings, one often feels that they are saying more than we can decipher. Yet one must avoid reading more than is written. The drawing does not tell all. It is a contribution, often an indispensable one, to our understanding of a problem that does not find verbal expression.

Black and white

Are there differences between the human figure as drawn by young black or white children?

This question has been put to me several times by those who, assuming the child is drawing a self-portrait, would expect the drawing to show the racial identification of the young artist. Specifically, I have been asked whether the black child shades the face or the figure. After examining literally hundreds of drawings, my answer is a decided NO insofar as young children are concerned. Both black and white represent the head by a clear circle into which they add the features. I dare say that even highly experienced observers would be unable to tell which drawings were by white and which by black preschool children. Not until adolescence are we likely to see in the drawings the shaded face that proclaims racial difference. I am writing in 1972 and in only one instance has a young child, age seven, drawn the figures with an Afro hairdo that clearly expresses their and his racial identification; but even in this unusual example, the face is clear.

It is not surprising to find that young children's drawings are racially undifferentiated. Young children relate to other young children as persons, responding positively to some and not to others;

the interplay has nothing to do with color. The child sees beyond surface attributes.

In her book, *Measurement of Intelligence by Drawings*, published in 1926, F. L. Goodenough included human figure drawings by 16 black children ranging in age from 6 years 5 months to 14 years 5 months. None of the figures has a darkened face or any other feature that distinguishes it from figures drawn by white children. Four of the figures drawn by boys have weapons. Evenly divided, two white boys and two black boys armed their figures.

In an article that appeared in *Psychiatry: Journal for the Study of Interpersonal Process*, Vol. 31, No. 1, Feb. 1968, entitled "Northern School Children under Segregation," R. Coles reports on his studies of the drawings of black and white school children during this current period of social conflict. He is impressed by the differences in representation of the human form. The children were between five and twelve years and attended "white" schools. The vast majority of northern black children portrayed violence or injury. Significantly, fewer than half of the southern black children drew anything of that nature—their northern brothers may have felt freer to express their anger and frustration. Another interesting observation related to the manner in which black children depicted their white classmates. These were drawn larger, with accentuated teeth and threatening arms. They drew themselves as smaller and with rudimentary upper extremities, often omitting the arms altogether, while ears were large to listen, and legs were ready to move. Whites were drawn standing pat and firm. Obviously, these differences in the drawings by school-age children reflect the "historical moment."

Allow me to repeat that in examining human figures drawn by hundreds of black and white preschool children, I have been unable to detect any differences that give me a better than pure-chance success in identifying the race of the artist. Whatever happens is not manifest until the child is at school.

Body image and perception

It may be said, then, that a concept of one's body image is essential for a valid perception of the Outside; that the concept evolves, arriving at greater complexity through a sequence of identifiable stages; that while the impetus to its development arises from within, the form that the body image will assume is dependent upon the interaction between intrinsic forces and the Outside; that by Outside is meant the child's personal environment, and that preeminent is the person who provides the affection and stimulation that is called "mothering."

The concept of individuality develops slowly as the child begins to discover his hands, feet, genitalia, and especially as he becomes able to crawl, creep, walk away from the care-taker. By age two, many are able to verbalize their individuality, often to the dismay of the elders, by resisting direction and using the first personal pronoun to stand squarely on two feet and defiantly announce, "I won't."

In this briefly stated sequence, one can identify two stages. During the first, a static phase, the child learns about the body and its parts. During the second, a dynamic phase, the child projects his body image into the environment, into space. This phase is crucial if the body image is to develop beyond a primitive level. "The maturing child perceives his body as a vehicle for motor performance" (Cratty and Sams). Gesell speaks of the organism as an "action system." Appropriate response to environmental stimuli requires that one be aware not only of one's body parts but of their continually changing position and form in space. It is through movement that a concept of the body image is developed. It is affected by all that affects one's emotional life. This dynamic concept of the body image is expressed by P. Schilder in these quotes: "There is a continual interchange between our own body and the body image of others." "It is in a continual state of flux, it is always changing."

The essential role of movement in development of body image is evident in children whose movements are impaired by cerebral palsy or other disabling affliction. Human figures drawn by these children reveal a defective, immature, often distorted concept. This difficulty in acquiring a valid concept of the body image is often compounded by the sensory impairments that may be associated with organic cerebral pathology and that restrict the child's sources of information.

3

COGNITION

The drawings as expressions of intellectual maturity
Role of the image in cognition

The drawings as expressions of intellectual maturity

The first important work on children's drawings appeared in 1887 with the publication in Bologna of a tiny volume, *L'Arte dei Bambini*, by C. Ricci, an eminent art historian and critic. Interest in the subject developed rapidly throughout the western world. It soon led to the discovery of stages or sequences in the graphic expression of what observers in France, England, the United States, Germany, and Norway recognized as the child's favorite theme: the human figure. It all starts with scribbling, which W. Stern perceptively related to drawing as babbling is to speech. Then one day, at about age three and a half, the child makes a chance discovery that a form scribbled evokes a form perceived. What follows has been described by G. Rouma in a classic work that appeared in Paris in 1913. After reviewing studies by Ricci, Sully (1898), Roubier (1901), Barnes (1893), Partridge (1897), Levinstein (1897), Kerschensteiner (1903), Claparède (1906), Lamprecht (1906), Bencini (1908), and others, Rouma describes his own personal findings. The six stages he has identified have been confirmed repeatedly down to the present day. According to Rouma, the human schema evolves in the following order:

1. earliest attempts at representation resulting in an unrecognizable configuration;
2. the "tadpole" stage (*bonhomme têtard, Kopffüssler*, cephalopod, *etapa celula*) in which the human schema consists of legs issuing from a disproportionately large head;
3. transitional phase during which the cephalopod acquires a trunk and additional features;
4. full-face drawing of the person with progressive addition of body parts;
5. transitional stage during which early attempts at portraying profile may result in a mixed profile (both eyes present, two noses), head in profile while body and limbs are in frontal view, both arms issuing from one side of a frontal trunk;
6. correct profile orientation, a prelude to the depiction of movement.

It was evident that the progressions from stage to stage were an expression of maturation. In 1913, G. H. Luquet showed that the child's drawings represented a logical realism and not an attempt to draw what was seen by the eye. The external object was simply a cue; what the child drew was his internal model. In fact, the young child will draw a person in the same manner whether a subject is present or whether he is drawing from memory. Young children draw what they know, not what they see. Their realism was said to be intellectual, not visual.

The next step was to relate the evolution of the human figure to progressions in age and intellectual maturity. This task was undertaken by F. Goodenough, who devised the first scale for an evaluation of human figure drawings as expressions of mental age. The test found wide acceptance in the United States because of its attractiveness to children, ease of administration, permanence of the response for future comparison, and the high degree of correlation with standard IQ tests. In 1963, D. B. Harris revised it and established separate norms for boys and girls. Between 1963 and 1965, the test, generally known as the Goodenough-Harris Drawing Test, was given to a representative national sample of over 7,000 United States children. As a result, further refinements were recommended in a 1970 publication of the National Center for Health Statistics.

Role of the image in cognition

In their recent book, *Mental Imagery in the Child*, J. Piaget and B. Inhelder report on their ingenious, rigorously controlled study of the role of imagery in cognition. They discuss two contrasting hypotheses: one, which views knowledge as copy, attributes primary importance to the image; the other considers the role of the image to be symbolic, indispensable but subordinate to the operational dynamisms whereby the person assimilates knowledge by acting upon the image. In this latter hypothesis, proposed by the authors, cognition is attained only when the image has been subjected to an intellectual operation. The object can be known only by being conceptualized.

Piaget and Inhelder identify two stages in the evolution of imagery. In the first, the images are static. It is usually not until the child is about seven or eight that he is able to foresee sequences and thereby imagine movement, a stage that the authors call "imaginal anticipation." Incidentally, it is at that age that children are able to depict movement. A bright child might arrive at the second stage at a younger age. The important point is the succession, static then anticipatory; the ages are subject to individual variation.

4

BEYOND COGNITION

**The drawings express more than intellectual maturity
Limitations of the Goodenough-Harris Drawing Test
Drawings by the neurologically impaired
The need for a developmental perspective**

The drawings express more than intellectual maturity

While justifiably emphasizing the value of drawings as expressions of general intelligence, neither Goodenough nor Harris has sufficiently recognized their affective and perceptuo-motor aspects, since these do not lend themselves to the same degree of objectivity and measurement as does their cognitive aspect. To date, there is no qualitative scale that has met with acceptance and reliability comparable to the Goodenough-Harris scale.

Goodenough recognizes that evidence of instability may sometimes be expressed in the drawings even before clinical manifestations become apparent.

Harris, taking a more rigidly scientific stance, is less willing to concede other than cognitive values to the drawings. He does not consider them valuable as measures of personality factors.

As mentioned earlier, W. Wolff was not satisfied with the statement that children drew what they knew, not what they saw. He insisted that the most important element was being left out: the emotional factor.

The drawings were being viewed as expressions of a body image that is shaped by external as well as maturational influences. Among the external influences, prime importance was attributed to the parental figures. A third dimension in organization of body image was conceded to perceptual processes in which sensation and movement were inextricably interwoven.

As manifestations of the body image, human figure drawings may be regarded as a distillation of the cognitive, affective, and perceptual complex from which that image is derived. It follows that the drawing of a person by an emotionally disturbed or neurologically impaired child will tend to differ from that by one who is well adjusted and neurologically intact. Direct observation has, indeed, shown this to be so and has led to the inclusion of human figure drawings in the diagnostic work-up, especially when cerebral dysfunction and emotional disorders are suspected. In this connection, I cannot but reaffirm the view expressed by Machover that those who have had intimate experience with the drawings consider them indispensable.

In 1959, N. D. Sundberg undertook a survey to determine which tests were most used in clinical work. The sources of information were psychological and mental health services throughout the United States. The Rorschach ranked first among 62 tests reported and immediately following was the Draw-a-Person Test.

Comparison with earlier surveys conducted in 1935 and 1946 revealed a sharp increase in the use of projective techniques and specifically in the recognition given the D-A-P Test.

Limitations of the Goodenough-Harris Drawing Test

As the test came into general use, numerous instances were noted in which mental age as expressed by the human figure drawing did not correspond to that derived from the Stanford-Binet and other well-standardized tests of intelligence. At first, the discrepancy cast a shadow on the validity of the Draw-a-Person Test. But some investigators took a different approach and sought an explanation for the conflicting finding. In 1940, L. Bender, noting the discrepancy between Goodenough mental age and Stanford-Binet score in drawings by the neurologically impaired, attributed the fact to a defective concept of the body image. As a result, the drawing would be substantially inferior to what one would expect of an unimpaired child of comparable age and intelligence. Bender saw the implications of the findings not only as an aid to diagnosis of brain damage but also as suggesting therapy that could help the child to develop an adequate body image. Failing this, the child would continue to perceive the environment in a distorted way.

Another source of error in estimating intellectual maturity from the Goodenough-Harris Test is traceable to those children whose concept of body image is defective, distorted, or disorganized because of emotional disorder. During the first decade of this century, publications were appearing in France on the art of the mentally deranged. Dealing more specifically with emotional disturbance in the young, Rouma showed how the spontaneous drawings could be used in studies of emotionally disturbed children and how the drawings might reveal the genesis of the disorder. In 1949, K. Machover's *Personality Projection in the Drawing of the Human Figure* set the stage for qualitative assessment of the drawings as indicators of emotional conflict.

A quarter century of experience in administering the Draw-a-Person Test has convinced me that when the result fails to match the child's intellectual capacity, the reason for the discrepancy is to be sought either in an intrinsic neurological dysfunction or in extrinsic factors that have adversely affected the child's emotional life. In both instances, the basic problem is an immature, impaired, or disorganized concept of the body image.

The diagnostic implications of this sensitive test are obvious. But can the drawings do more than indicate what is usual and what is not, what is normal and what is deviant? Can they differentiate the emotionally disturbed from the neurologically impaired? Are there specific qualitative differences between the two?

Drawings by the neurologically impaired

What features distinguish these drawings from all others? To answer that question one must study the drawings of children who are centrally impaired and who do not present with emotional disorder or intellectual deficit severe enough to contaminate the sample. Such pure cases are, indeed, more hypothetical than real. One will have to be content with those subjects whose predominant difficulty is neurological and whose associated problems are not contributing significantly to their handicap. It follows that the answer to the question posed in the beginning will not be clear-cut.

The term "neurologically impaired" shall be used to designate those with brain dysfunction resulting from demonstrable organic etiology—that is, those children in whom the diagnosis of organicity is not merely assumed (as in so-called minimal brain dysfunction) but supported by unequivocal neurological findings on clinical examination, X-ray studies of the brain, or clearly abnormal brain-wave patterns.

L. Bender was the first to report on human figure drawings by children whose brains had been affected by encephalitis. In 1940, she called attention to the aforementioned discrepancy between intelligence and concept of body image as reflected in the human figure drawings. Her observation has been subsequently and repeatedly confirmed by numerous investigators, including the present writer. But while there is general recognition that the drawings are inferior, the same cannot be said for attempts to identify specific features that clearly differentiate them from those by children who are emotionally disturbed. I believe that part of the problem resides in terminology. The same or similar terms are often applied to both groups: "distorted," "bizarre," "grotesque," "disorganized." These general, ill-defined terms confuse the issue. The images they evoke are much too vague to be meaningful. This is especially so with "grotesque" and "bizarre"; probably less so with "distorted" and "disorganized." Personally, I prefer the following terms to designate what recurs in the drawings by brain-damaged children: "immature concept of body image," "perseveration," "poor planning" (drawing without considering beforehand whether the figure will fit into the available space), "impulsivity" (rapid, slapdash execution), "going out-of-bounds" (drawing off the paper), "uninhibited" (uncontrolled, random activity), "poor coordination" (overlapping of lines or lines that do not meet, poor control over the writing instrument), and "tendency to revert to scribbling." Attempts have been made to arrive at greater specificity by noting "asymmetry," "slanting at an angle of more than 15 degrees," "arms incorrectly attached," "incorrect number of fingers." These observations may have validity if considered within the framework of the child's developmental age, since all of the traits are common, usual, and therefore normal during the pre-school years.

While recognizing the distinctive features that often help in differentiating drawings by the neurologicaly impaired, I believe that their validity is tied to the skill and experience of the examiner. One is not dealing with a homogeneous population nor with a single clinical entity. Each brain-damaged child is impaired in his own way. Because of this great variability, norms are not available. Brain dysfunction and neurological impairment are broad concepts embracing a spectrum of disorders varying in kind and in intensity. Among these are cerebral palsy, symptomatic epilepsy, expanding lesions, localized damage, metabolic disorders, aphasia, and other less clearly defined abnormalities that interfere with function at various levels of integration. Hence, disorders of sense, motion, perception, and thinking.

The quantification achieved in measuring intellectual maturity from human figure drawings cannot be applied in assessing neurological and emotional aspects, for in these the indicators are qualitative.

Diagnosis of emotional disorder or neurological impairment must not rest upon the drawings alone. These are but one in a constellation of signs that will have to be discovered in order to meet the diagnostic criterion. For some of us, the drawings are an indispensable item in a comprehensive examination. No sensible clinician would diagnose Down's syndrome from the mere fact that the child has simian creases in his palms.

In diagnosing cerebral dysfunction, I have found it most helpful to supplement the Draw-a-Person Test with other drawing items aimed at uncovering perceptuo-motor difficulty. Bender's Visual Motor Gestalt Test is widely used with school-age children.

Most normal children can copy the forms satisfactorily by age ten. At younger age levels, I have the children copy simple geometric forms: a cross, square, divided rectangle, triangle. Those with demonstrable cerebral pathology have difficulty reproducing the configurations at age-level expectations. Their attempts usually result in crude, distorted, rotated forms or in utter failure.

The need for a developmental perspective

Valid appraisal of a child's drawing is not possible without taking into account the age and developmental level.

Omission of parts of the body is often indicative of feelings and personality traits. And indeed, the omission of hands is certainly noteworthy because of their symbolic role as agents of aggression as well as a means for physically reaching out to explore the environment, to attack, and to caress.

The significance of omission and exaggeration depends upon the level at which the child is functioning. An enormous head at four and five is quite usual. Omission of arms and hands at five—an age when many children do not include these among the eight parts usually represented—should not be viewed in the same light as their omission later on. We do not expect arms at four; we may see them at five; we expect them after six.

A disorganized, unrecognizable scribble that is called "a man" is quite normal at three but not so at five.

A mixed profile, with both eyes and two noses, is often seen as a transitional phase between full-face and profile representation. It is a developmental phase along the continuum toward the visual realism that is usually seen between seven and nine years, when the child with increasing consistency will attempt to draw what he sees with his eye.

5

CHILDREN'S DRAWINGS
AS A PROJECTIVE TECHNIQUE

Display of feelings and personality traits
Security and insecurity expressed graphically
Omission of upper extremities
Accentuated hands and fingers
Small, unsupportive feet
Exaggerated size of a parent
Concealment of the genital area
Explicit portrayal of the genitalia
Sex role confusion
Figure drawings as evidence of homosexuality

Display of feelings and personality traits

Paradoxically consistent yet ever changing, the body image is sensitively reactive to influences that disturb the emotional life. Insofar as human figure drawing represents a concept of body image as experienced at that time, it will tend to express, unconsciously and symbolically, the hurt that is making the child painfully aware of his feelings. As his thoughts are turned inward, the drawing becomes a more intimately personal statement. Depending upon the degree of turmoil, the body image and its graphic representation may be sweepingly or focally affected, thoroughly disrupted or different from the usual in only a particular, and in any gradient between these two extremes.

Among the more pervasive deviations are scatter of body parts, absence of persons in a scene, striking incongruities, defacement of a just-drawn human figure, rigid robot-like figures. These may be observed in the drawings of seriously disturbed children.

Neurotic behavior and feelings of inadequacy may be expressed by drawing small figures, often at the lower margin of the page where they stand on tiny unstable feet, exaggerated size of a domineering parent figure, excessive shading, explicit portrayal of genitalia, concealment of the genital area, sex role confusion, emphasis or omission of arms and hands, darkened clouds and darkened sun.

Examples of the above-mentioned items will be offered. Expressions of feeling states as portrayed in family drawings will be treated in a subsequent chapter.

Security and insecurity expressed graphically

Insecure, anxious children tend to draw small figures that timidly occupy only a small area of the available space.

In contrast, the secure, well adjusted child will draw freely, with joyful abandon, creating a figure that expresses, by its size, sweep, and conspicuous placement on the page, freedom from inhibiting anxiety.

FIGURE 13

Drawn by an insecure girl, age 7½. Timid, lacking in self-esteem. Fatherless home. Tense, anxious mother. Underachievement at school, despite fully average intelligence. As she drew she repeatedly asked, "Am I doing O.K.?" She said the figure represented "me" (herself).

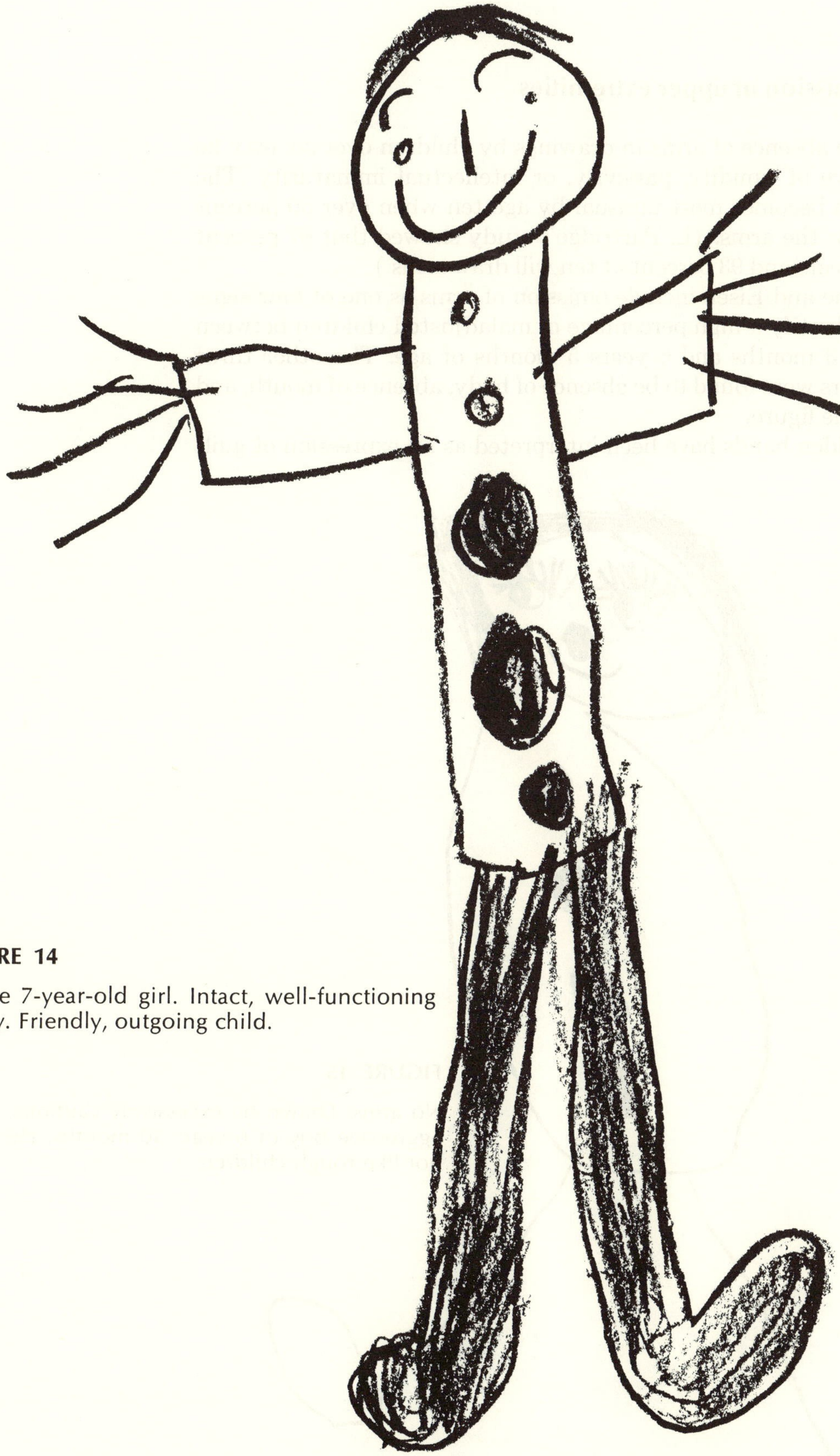

FIGURE 14

Secure 7-year-old girl. Intact, well-functioning family. Friendly, outgoing child.

Omission of upper extremities

The absence of arms in drawings by children over six may be indicative of timidity, passivity, or intellectual immaturity. The omission becomes most unusual by age ten when over 90 percent will draw the arms. (L. Partridge's study showed that 67 percent at five years and 93 percent at ten will draw arms.)

Vane and Eisen include omission of arms as one of four signs which identify a high percentage of maladjusted children between 5 years 3 months and 6 years 5 months of age. The other three indicators were found to be absence of body, absence of mouth, and grotesque figure.

Hidden hands have been interpreted as an expression of guilt feelings.

FIGURE 15

No arms. Drawn by excessively cautious, non-aggressive boy of 6 years 10 months. He does not like rough children.

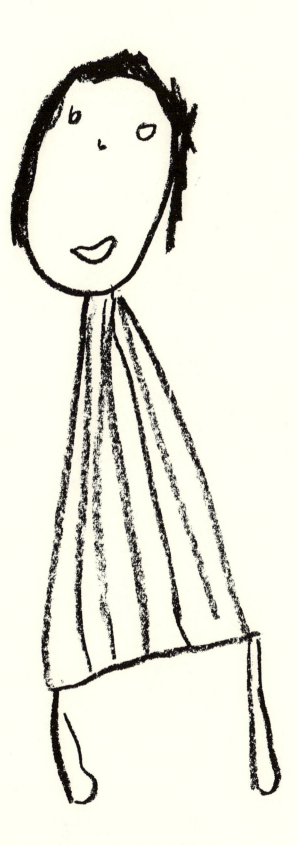

FIGURE 16

Drawn by a non-aggressive, retiring girl of 5 years 8 months. She said the figure represented herself.

FIGURE 17

The arms are omitted in this and the following drawings by a timid, non-aggressive child, a boy of 7 years. He is enuretic, upset if there is any change in his routine. Worries if a person is one minute late.

FIGURE 18

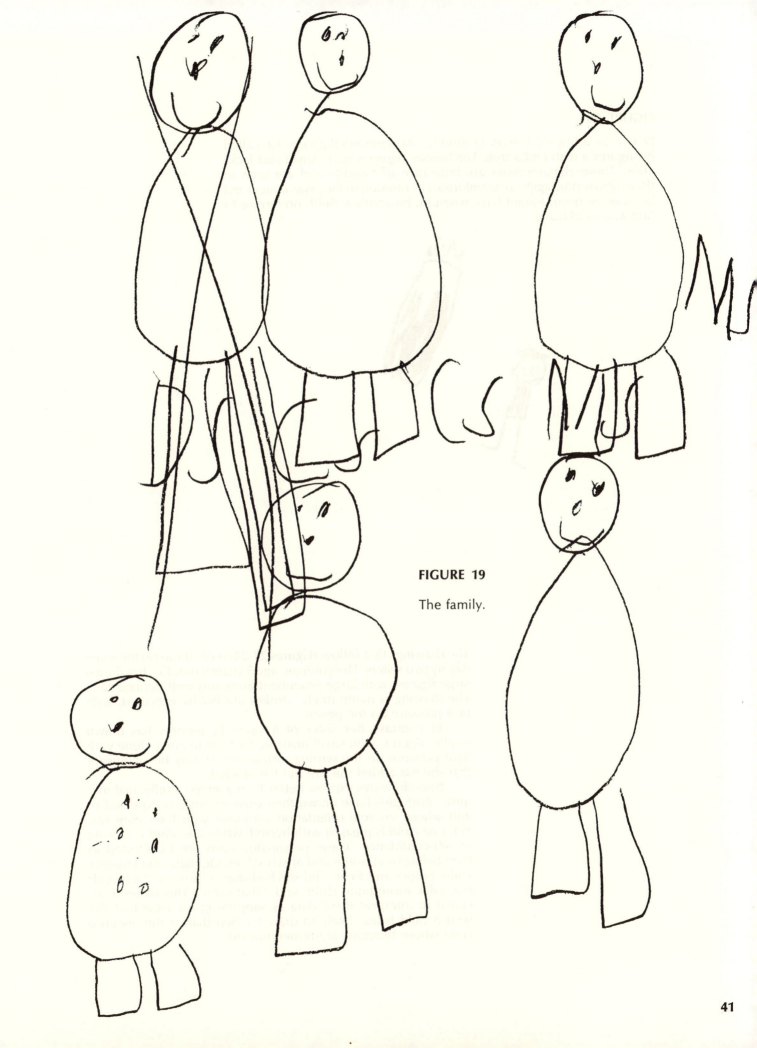

FIGURE 19

The family.

FIGURE 20

Drawn by a boy of 5 years 11 months. Average intelligence. He called his figures a man and a tree. The human figure is quite small and lacks arms. These characteristics are indicative of timidity and are seen in drawings by non-aggressive children. His mother, in fact, was concerned because he never fought back when hit by another child, preferring to turn away and leave.

The drawings that follow (**Figures 21-24**) were done on the same day by two sisters. The younger, age 5 years 9 months, has drawn large figures, with large prominent arms and well-defined feet. The drawing is made freely, strokes are boldly executed, with firm pressure on the pencil.

In contrast, her sister of 6 years 11 months has drawn smaller figures, with small unstable feet, small arms, done with light pressure on the writing instrument. It may be significant that she has added the sun but has shaded it.

Both drawings express better than average intellectual maturity. Both girls have drawn their own sex first, as expected of girls whose sex role orientation conforms with their core sex. Yet, one child is pleased with herself, while the other is lacking in self-confidence. These personality traits are manifested in their behavior at home and at school. Incidentally, the younger child, bolder and freer, said she had drawn "Joanne," a friend; the older, more timid child, said "That's me." This writer is inclined to interpret these data as supporting his view that the secure child is less likely to draw the Self than is the insecure child whose thoughts are turned inward.

FIGURE 21

FIGURE 22

FIGURE 23

FIGURE 24

Accentuated hands and fingers

Exaggerated size of hands is regarded as symbolic of aggressive tendencies if the figure is a self-portrait. When the figure represents a parent or care-taker, the emphasis on hands may indicate aggression received, anticipated or feared.

FIGURE 25

Drawn by a 7-year-old boy of superior intelligence, but maladjusted at home and at school. Seeks compensatory gratification through food and acquisition of objects. Stealing has been a frequent problem. Note the accentuated fingers.

45

FIGURE 26

Drawn by a boy, age 9 years 3 months. Average intelligence. Unassertive. Arms folded.

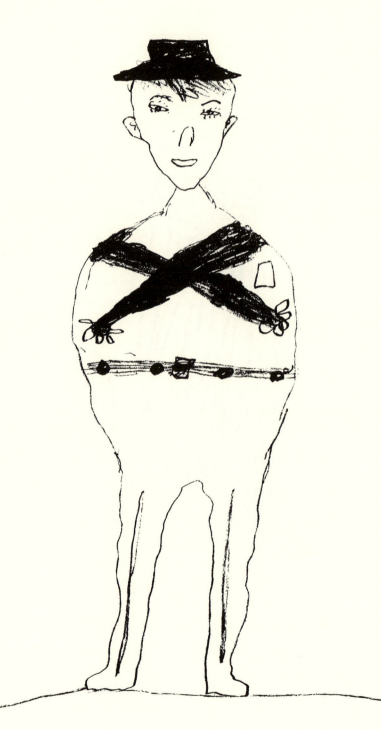

FIGURE 27

Drawn by boy, age 14 years 10 months. Underachiever at school. Stanford-Binet and WISC reveal average intelligence. Hands hidden. Note crotch.

Small, unsupportive feet

A frequent observation in the drawings of insecure children is the instability of the figure, tottering over the ineffectual support of tiny feet. The child unconsciously and symbolically expresses the instability of a personality structured upon a weak foundation. Lacking basic feelings of security the personality development is undermined; persistent anxiety continues to impede growth towards emotional maturity and mental health. In his book, *Childhood and Society*, E. Erikson has indicated how much depends upon the establishment of a basic sense of trust during the first year of life.

FIGURE 28

Drawn by an insecure, timid girl of 4 years 10 months. Responsive socially, excellent attention span, above-average intelligence. Seizure disorder and sensori-neural hearing loss. Fatherless home. Note the tiny upper extremities and tiny unstable feet.

Exaggerated size of a parent

When a child's image of a parent is of one who is domineering, overwhelming, aggressive, or frightening, the child will tend to draw that person larger than the others in a family group, regardless of actual physical dimensions. And so we see drawings in which one parent towers above another who is physically much taller and heavier. After all, the child is right in evaluating persons according to their significance and not by their bulk. The impressive parent may be portrayed with large hands if viewed as hostile and threatening. The ineffectual parent may be depicted with small or even absent hands.

FIGURE 29

Drawn by adopted boy, age 6 years 7 months. Mother is impressive. He has omitted to include himself in the family picture. Average intelligence. Attends first grade.

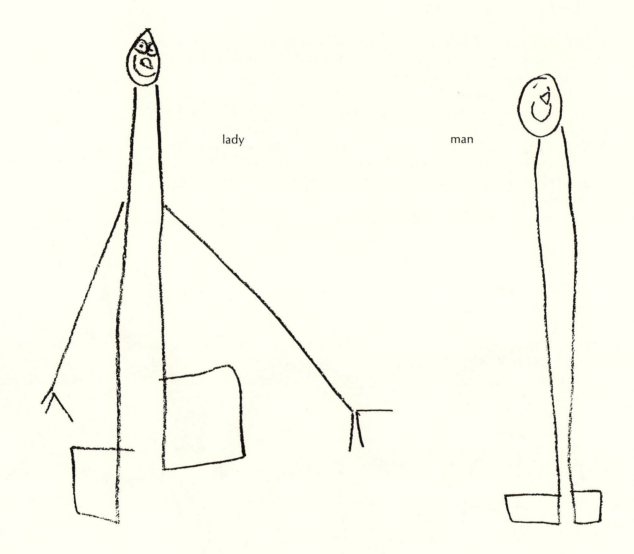

lady

man

FIGURE 30

These two figures were drawn within minutes of each other by a girl of 6 years 4 months, bright but emotionally immature and excessively dependent upon the mother who feeds, dresses her, and assists at toilet.

The "lady" has pupils, and accentuated arms and fingers. Mother is a domineering person. Judging from the emphasis on arms (totally lacking in the male figure), the child seems to view her as the aggressive parent.

Concealment of the genital area

This attitude of the human figure is often seen in drawings by adolescent girls. The female figure is drawn with hands demurely covering the lower abdomen, while the male figure has arms boldly outstretched. One girl drew a bride with a bouquet over the center of her body. Others may place objects over the lower abdomen. One girl drew her family, everyone doing something (K-F-D) but herself in bed withdrawn from the action, the lower half of her body covered by a blanket.

These features seem to be expressions of pudicity when not associated with behavior disorders.

Hiding the hands has been observed in drawings by children as expressions of guilt arising from masturbation.

Drawings by a bright girl of 8½ **(Figures 31-33)** express interest in reproduction (cats and kits); in marriage (bridegroom's arms demurely folded); note her own hands crossed in front in the family picture.

Cats and Kits

FIGURE 31

FIGURE 32

FIGURE 33

Explicit portrayal of the genitalia

In drawings by preadolescent children, sex differences are represented symbolically: by abundance of hair, eyelashes, ornaments, clothing in the female figure; and by shorter hair (even to this day), guns, pipes, ties in the male. It is so unusual to see the genitalia that their presence may be highly significant. Failure to add the sex organs does not seem to be due to cultural taboos. A more plausible explanation may be the shift of interest from his body to the fascinating world outside that marks behavior of the latency child. During the years from six to twelve, well adjusted children become increasingly involved in mastering new skills and in conforming to the mores of their schoolmates and friends. Obscene graffiti are generally at a higher level from the ground and are characteristically the work of older children.

In thousands of drawings by latency children, this writer has collected only half a dozen specimens in which penis or vulva has been clearly portrayed. The reasons for this unusual addition are to be found in experiences that have made the child precociously aware of the high emotional charge invested in the sex organs. Hernia operation or circumcision after infancy may have caused castration·fear. Seduction by older children or adults or more subtle maneuvers may have aroused feelings usually in abeyance during latency, especially in the bright, sensitive child. Whatever the reason, of the few cases that have come to the attention of this writer, most showed behavior disorders of one kind or another (aggression, phobias) but one was, and continues in adolescence to be, outgoing and well adjusted.

FIGURE 34

Female figure by a boy of 11. Though wearing pants, her sex is evident from the treatment of the eyes, the earrings, and above all from the unusual abundance of hair. In the lower right are scissors; a direct line connects them to the hair. The figure has large, powerful arms and long fingers, and accentuated pointed teeth. The boy seems to view the female as threatening. The scissors express his hostility.

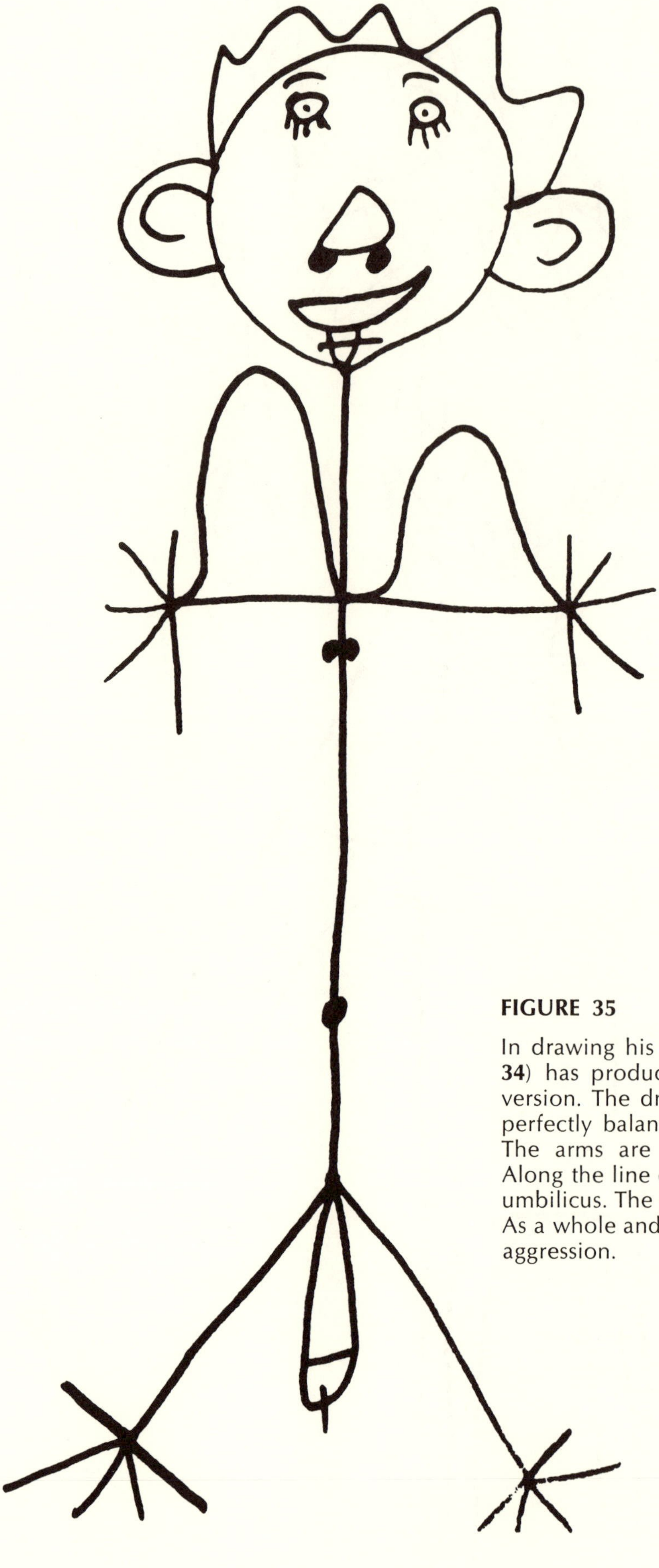

FIGURE 35

In drawing his own sex, the same boy (**Figure 34**) has produced this artistic, highly stylized version. The drawing is strikingly symmetrical, perfectly balanced, and reduced to essentials. The arms are endowed with huge muscles. Along the line of the trunk are the nipples and umbilicus. The penis is impressive and piercing. As a whole and in its parts, the figure expresses aggression.

Sex role confusion

People are most important in the lives of young children. It comes as no surprise that the great majority of children draw the human figure by preference. This fact has been noted by observers in many lands and in this and the past century. Another important finding, abundantly confirmed, is that children will draw a human figure of their own sex when asked to draw a person.

Two inferences may be drawn from these findings. First, that since the tendency to draw the human figure is dominant, failure to do so and to draw inanimate objects instead must be considered unusual, possibly deviant, suggesting difficulty in interpersonal relationships, abnormal disinterest, emotional detachment, autism. And second, since the vast majority of young children tend to draw their own sex, preferential drawing of the opposite sex suggests the possibility of sex role confusion, of failure to assume a sex role corresponding to the biological sex.

A variety of reasons may account for the unusual preference. Children reared in institutions, cared for consistently and exclusively by female personnel, have no opportunity to learn the ways of the male. Boys in their own family but under the thumb of a domineering mother, or girls in homes where the father is tyrannical and mother abjectly and passively subservient, may identify with the more impressive parent. Then there are children who, for no apparent reason, are manifesting already in their preschool years an uncommon interest in what the culture has assigned to the opposite sex. The tomboy is usually not so disturbing to parents as is the male child who habitually dons female clothing and plays with dolls instead of trains and soldiers.

The years from three to six are probably the most decisive for the establishment of masculinity or femininity. Human figure drawings will reflect psychosexual orientation to an increasing degree as the child matures. At first, sex differences will be indicated by hair length (even today, despite the current trend towards unisex). Later, there will appear differences in clothing, though trousers are now beginning to confound the situation. Differences in body contour, special attention to eyes, ornaments, and hairdos appear in female figures by subteen and adolescent girls. Male figures drawn by boys tend to exhibit attempts to portray movement while some may carry guns, cigarettes, or other objects to which sexual symbolism is attached. Intelligent, perceptive sophisticates will portray sex differences at an earlier age.

Contrary to what younger children do, adolescent girls may draw a male figure first instead of their own sex. This occurs frequently and is an expression of interest, not of identification.

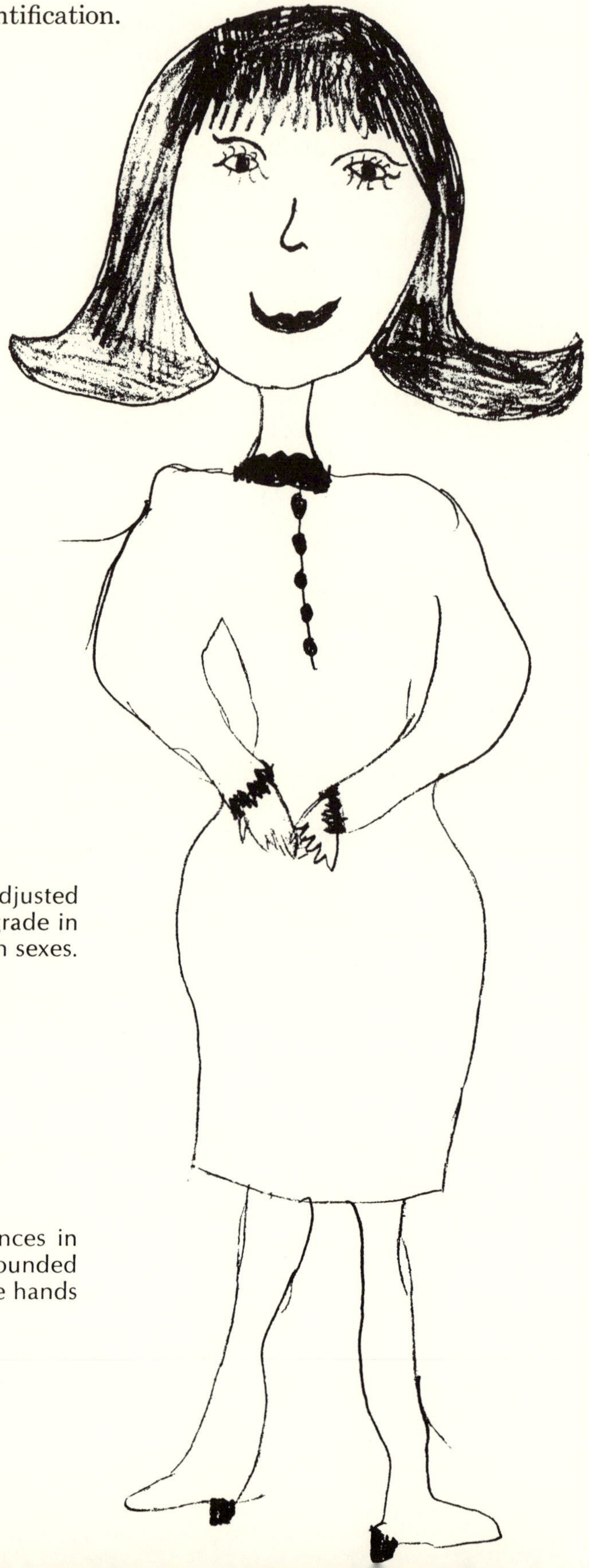

Depiction of sex differences **(Figures 36, 37)** by a well-adjusted adolescent girl of 12 years 10 months. She attends 7th grade in a coed school. Good student. Popular with peers of both sexes. Menarche at age 10 years 6 months.

FIGURE 36

Female drawing shows sex differences in hair styling, treatment of eyes, rounded hips, lipstick, dress, and heels. Note hands over lower abdomen.

FIGURE 37

Male drawing shows male clothing (shirt and trousers), shorter hair, no eyelashes, no lipstick. Note that the arms are extended.

Sex role confusion is evident in **Figure 38,** drawn by a boy of 5½ years. He has been living in an institution since he was 10 days old. As is generally the case, the attendant personnel is female. Except for brief encounters with male physicians, social workers, and maintenance employees, his world is female. Having had little opportunity to relate to a grown male, the child has spontaneously drawn a female figure that he calls Kate, a nurse.

FIGURE 38

FIGURE 39

Asked to draw a person, a boy of 4 years 6 months produced this female figure. He prefers to play with female dolls and dons his mother's undergarments. This drawing is superior to the next one, a male figure

FIGURE 40

When the boy had drawn his first human figure, a female, the examiner said, "Now draw a boy." This is the male figure, inferior both qualitatively and quantitatively when compared with his previous female figure.

Numerous studies have shown that a boy's concept of masculinity is impeded in fatherless homes, or where the father is present but ineffectual.

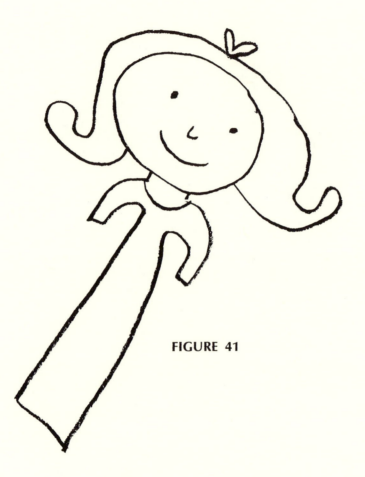

FIGURE 41

In **Figure 41** a boy of 7, physically normal and of average intelligence, has been asked to draw a person. He draws a female instead of a person of his own sex. His parents separated when he was 4. He is cared for by his maternal grandmother while mother is away at work. He rarely sees his father. The environment is exclusively female. There is no opportunity for a relationship with a grown male. Mother is disturbed because he dresses in female clothing—her undergarments if he can get them—and prefers to play with girls and their dolls. In **Figure 42,** as his three best wishes, he has drawn a heart, a flower, and a clover, hardly what one would expect from a boy.

FIGURE 42

A boy of 12 years 11 months **(Figures 43, 44),** a foster child in a mother-dominated home, getting psychotherapy because of enuresis, lying, poor adjustment at school, and for having run away from the foster home, and truancy, has a performance IQ of 75 and a verbal of 99 on the WISC. Rorschach indicates immaturity, depressed feelings of smallness, inadequacy. Perception of reality seems fairly good; deep seated problem in relation to the maternal figure. The natural mother is in the picture and, because of his behavior in the foster home, has reluctantly agreed to take him back. Asked to draw a person, the boy first drew an imposing female figure; he was then asked to draw a man. The female has hands, the male none. Sex differences are minimal for a boy of his age.

FIGURE 43   **FIGURE 44**

Sex role confusion is strikingly revealed in two drawings **(Figures 45, 46)** by an adolescent female pseudohermaphrodite. She was reared as a girl from early childhood. Her first response to the Draw-a-Person Test is the female figure suggesting her identification with that sex. She then drew a male. The two figures are practically identical except for more elaborate treatment of hair in the female. But both have broad shoulders and narrow hips and minimal differences in clothing. Both are drawn with timid, light, broken lines, small hands and tiny feet—all features that indicate insecurity. She is most reluctant to discuss her problem and she has omitted the mouth in both her figures.

FIGURE 45

FIGURE 46

Figure drawings as evidence of homosexuality

Grams and Rinder have attempted to clarify the issue by examining the drawings of "homosexual" delinquent boys and comparing them with drawings by "non-homosexual" delinquent boys. As a basis for their investigation they tested signs indicated by Machover as significant. Among these are drawing of the female figure first, emphasis on hips and buttocks, failure to draw "V" of crotch, and other less explicit but symbolic features, such as shading of lips, eyelashes, large ears and nose. Their study failed to prove validity for any of the signs or for the 15 signs taken collectively.

The conclusions drawn are unconvincing when one considers the criterion used in classifying the boys as homosexual or not. Having engaged in homosexual acts under conditions of confinement in an institution does not rule out a preference for a heterosexual partner under more normal conditions of freedom and availability.

The signs listed by Machover from clinical experience are surely suggestive if not diagnostic or predictive.

6

MANIFESTATIONS OF

EMOTIONAL DISORDER

Scatter of body parts
Grotesque, bizarre figures
Scribbling over the drawn human figure
Rigid, robot-like figures
Excessive shading
Drawings without persons
Dark clouds and darkened sun
Psychobiological mutism
The "squiggle game"

Scatter of body parts

This is certainly unusual and deviant, since the vast majority of children, even from their earliest attempts at representing a person, will draw an integrated figure. Even when the person is only a head, the child will place the features within the primal circle, not scattered about. Later on when, during the tadpole stage, the person is head and limbs, these issue directly from the head and with it form a whole. Clearly, a human figure drawing in which the parts are scattered with no relation to each other is a deviation from the norm. This failure to produce a unitary figure has been noted in seriously disturbed children and is indicative of their own disorganized personality.

With favorable response to therapy, gradual integration of the personality will be reflected in corresponding approximation of body parts in the drawings. Preserving the drawings will allow comparison with subsequent productions, thereby helping to evaluate changes that may have occurred in personality.

FIGURE 47

Figures 47 and 48 are by a girl in a foster home where she had been exposed to adult sexual activity and main-line heroin addiction. Body parts are scattered. She named them eyes, big nose, hands, feet, and hair. Chronological age: 5 years 10 months.

FIGURE 48

FIGURE 49

Scatter of body parts. Emotionally disturbed child of 5 years.

Grotesque, bizarre figures

These terms are admittedly vague, yet how else are we to designate the striking incongruities and distortions that render the drawings so queerly different from the usual and normative.

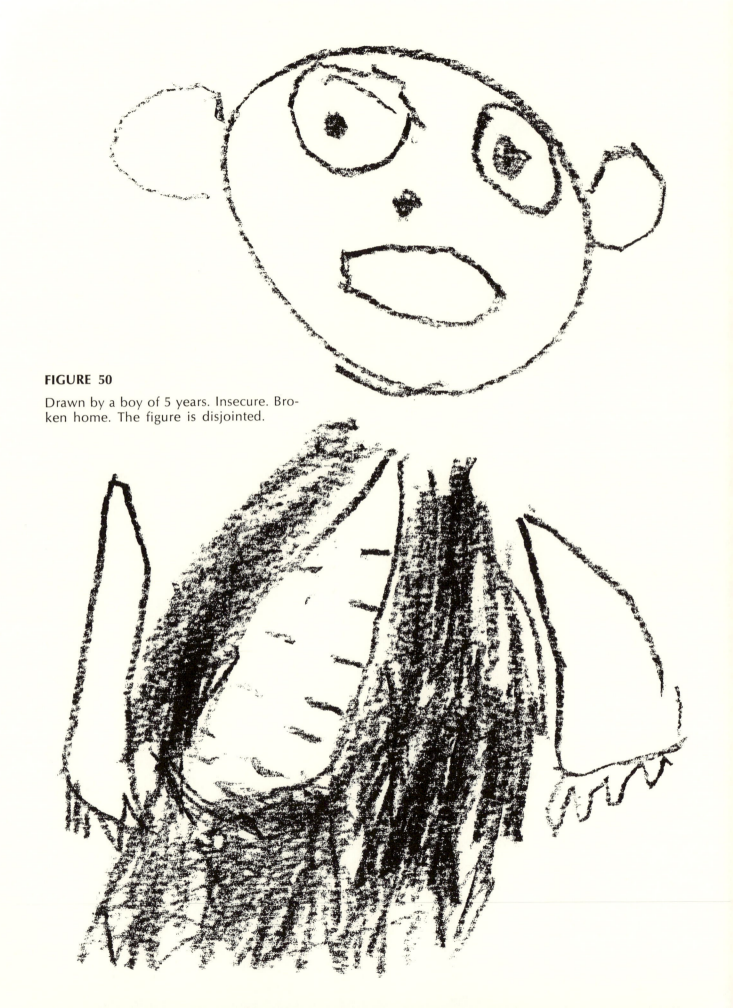

FIGURE 50

Drawn by a boy of 5 years. Insecure. Broken home. The figure is disjointed.

FIGURE 51

Drawn by a girl, age 6 years 2 months. Insecure. Excessively fearful of the unfamiliar.

FIGURE 52

Drawn by a boy of 9 years. Phobias and compulsive behavior. Also signs of cerebral dysfunction.

FIGURE 53

Drawn by same boy as **Figure 52**.

FIGURE 54

Drawn by boy, age 12 years 10 months. Very inferior school work. Foster child, in deplorable home.

Scribbling over the drawn human figure

In **Figure 55,** a girl of 5 years 6 months has drawn a female figure, head, eyes, pupils, nose, mouth, dress, arms, fingers, legs, feet. She then scribbles vigorously over her drawing in an attempt to obliterate it. The child's drawing is above average for her age. She has a sensori-neural hearing loss as a result of maternal rubella. Parents separated, there was much tension in the home. Mother is domineering. The child is socially responsive but predominantly involved with things. She is the older of two children. Mother is at home and receives public assistance supplement. A teacher in charge of the parent education program has noted a highly charged atmosphere in the home where "emotion is splattered all over". The drawing may be interpreted as expressing strongly negative feelings.

FIGURE 55

75

Rigid, robot-like figures

Stiff, stereotyped figures are drawn by children who may act out their difficulties in a variety of ways. But though there is no uniformity in the form that the disorder may assume, there is one problem that is common to most of the children: a discrepancy between ability and performance at school. Many are bright yet doing poorly academically. Emotional immaturity is a constant finding. Often the problem can be traced to a home atmosphere marked by excessive tension.

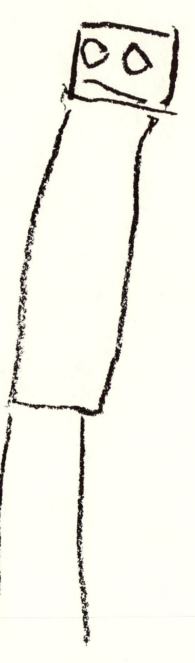

FIGURE 56

Drawn by a boy, chronological age 4 years 6 months. Bright child. Nonaggressive, will walk away or talk his way out ("You're my friend") when peers are rough with him. Vague digestive disorders. Allergies. Tense family situation. The figure is geometric and it has no arms.

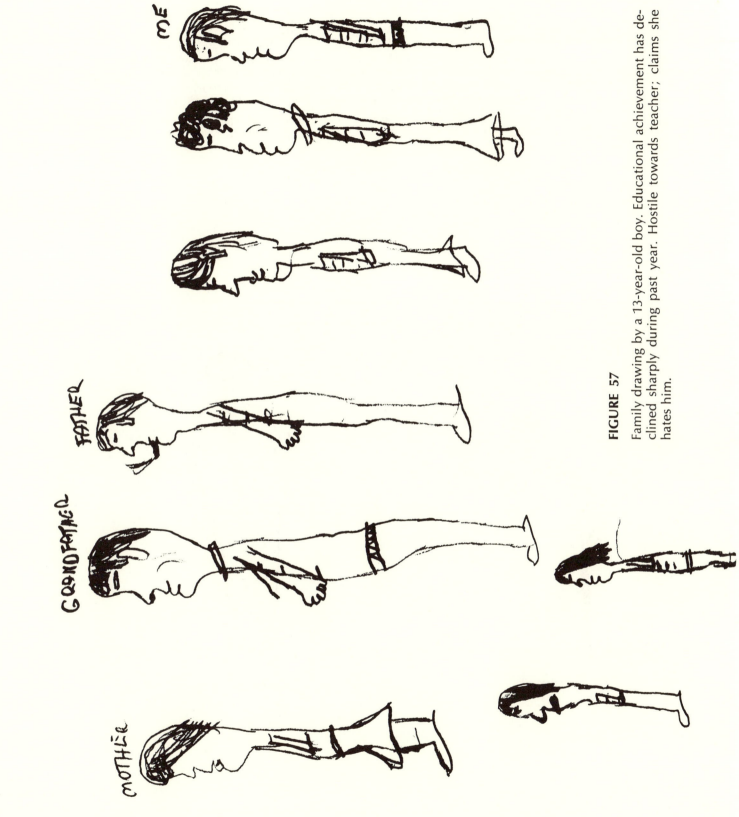

FIGURE 57

Family drawing by a 13-year-old boy. Educational achievement has declined sharply during past year. Hostile towards teacher; claims she hates him.

77

Figures 58 and 59 are by an adopted 11-year-old boy. Average general intelligence. Poorly motivated. Underachiever. School work unsatisfactory. Pessimistic, discouraged attitude. Enuretic. Poor self-image. Says "I'm the dumbest." Concerned over adoption. Recently said to adoptive mother, "Do you mean somebody had me and just gave me away?" Human figure drawings reveal immature concept of body image. Practically no difference between male and female figures. Male has shorter hair, that's all.

man

FIGURE 58

lady

FIGURE 59

Excessive shading

Emphasis on shading parts or the totality of the drawn figure has repeatedly been observed in drawings by anxious children. The shading may be limited to the face, to the lower half of the body, or more specifically to the genital area.

I have already alluded to the fact that young black children do not shade the face, unless they too, like their white peers, are expressing anxiety. This may stem from preoccupation with their body image, identity, or it may express their concern over parental discord and family disruption.

Machover observed excessive, vigorous shading, at times directed at the genital area, in drawings by repressed, overly controlled young school children, at an age when latency would be expected.

I have observed unhappy children to shade the sun, and one sexually precocious child to shade the window in a room in which a large bed occupies the conspicuous center of the drawing.

In connection with shading, it is relevant to note that in Rorschach protocols shading responses are indicative of anxiety. According to Ames, Métraux and Walker, who have reported on developmental trends from early childhood through adolescence, shading responses are unusual in latency children, reaching a peak at age thirteen, when the child tends to become introspective and concerned about his abilities. Such responses in much younger children may be indicative of emotional disturbance.

In **Figure 60,** a 6-year-old boy has drawn his family. He is an adopted child. Though bright, he has become increasingly disruptive at school. He is concerned over his origins and his status in the home. Feelings towards the adoptive mother are strongly ambivalent. There is another adopted younger boy in the home. The boys get along well. In the drawing, he has depicted from left to right, his brother, himself, father, and mother. In describing the two parental figures, drawn at the end, he said "My mother is kicking my father."

FIGURE 60

Drawings without persons

In accordance with the principle that children draw what is important to them, the human figure has been and continues to be their favorite subject. This observation made in the latter part of the nineteenth century by Ricci, Lukens, and subsequently by Ballard (England), Eng (Norway), Mühle (Germany), and Goodenough (United States), remains valid even in this age of technological miracles.

As the child grows in intellect and personality, the figure is destined to undergo a series of transformations but continues, at least throughout latency, to be ubiquitously present as a central motif in scenes that may include pets, a house, flowers, a tree, the radiant sun—perhaps a cloud or two.

It is so unusual for young children to omit persons from their drawings as to justify consideration of probable difficulty in interpersonal relationships.

As noted by Eng, children will transfer their previously acquired human schema onto their drawings of animals. The result is a four-legged creature with a human face.

FIGURE 61

Drawn by a boy of average intelligence, age 6 years 9 months. Adopted. Said it represented "a lady holding a dog, walking outside." The dog has a human face.

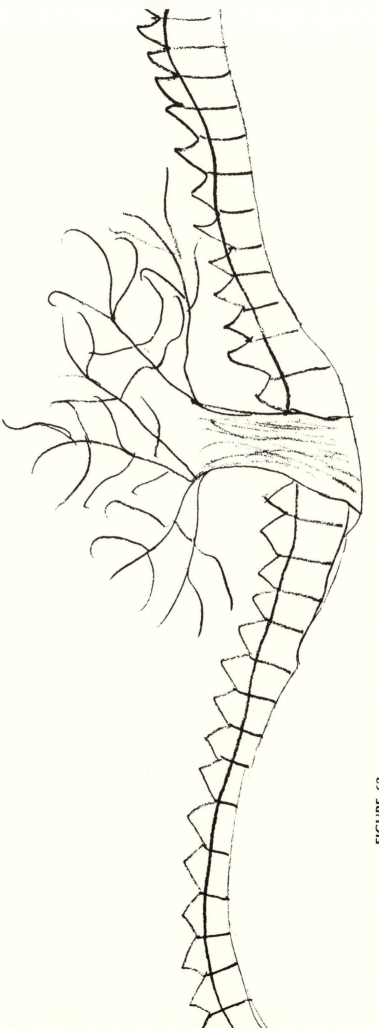

FIGURE 62

Drawn by a bright but unhappy girl of 12 years 10 months. She will not sleep alone because of an obsessive fear of death. The scene is bleak with its barren tree, clouds, fence. There are no persons.

83

Dark clouds and darkened sun

Many well adjusted children will brighten their human figure drawing by the addition of a radiant sun. This is usually in one of the upper corners of the paper often in the form of an arc. Issuing from its circumference are lines representing rays, and the sun may have a smiling face. It is interesting to observe that children from many and distant lands will draw the sun in exactly the same way, as though they had gotten together and agreed upon it.

It is unusual for children to add storm clouds and to darken the sun. These ominous signs have been seen in drawings by unhappy children.

Figure 63, which might very appropriately be titled "Tristesse," is the spontaneous drawing by an unhappy, unmotivated girl of 11. She is doing poorly at school despite average intelligence. She is not getting along well with her peers. Her anxiety is related to the home situation: her parents have separated. She has drawn a desolate scene: falling leaves, dark clouds overhead, no persons.

FIGURE 63

FIGURE 64

Drawn by a girl of 9. Dark sky. Darkened
sun. No persons.

Psychobiological mutism

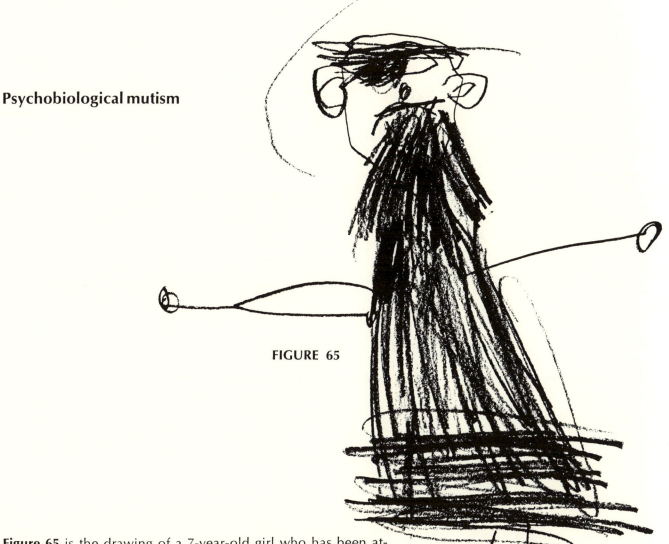

FIGURE 65

Figure 65 is the drawing of a 7-year-old girl who has been attending a school for the deaf because of failure to develop speech, originally attributed to sensori-neural hearing loss. Continued observation and lack of response to auditory and speech training over an extended period have indicated the need to review the original diagnostic impression. Audiometry is unreliable and equivocal in its results.

The child has a slender, wispy build, a far-away look, large, unblinking stary eyes, an angelic expression that hardly varies except for a faint smile in response to intensive social stimulation. She is cooperative but passive and totally lacking in initiative. It is not difficult to establish and to maintain eye contact. Her rapport with parents, teachers, and peers is uniformly shallow. General level of functioning is in the 6-year range.

She spontaneously drew this picture indicating by gesture that it was me. One of the first parts she drew was my beard. The figure has head, eyes, nose, mouth, ears (with holes), beard, body, arms, hand, legs, feet. It expresses quantitatively a 6-year intellectual maturity. On completing it she vigorously began to shade the trunk and part of the face. Excessive shading is a feature of all her drawings. It is interpreted as an indicator of anxiety. This drawing supports the impression derived from her behavior and the failure to benefit from amplification and training, that her mutism is not simply due to hearing impairment (if such there be in her case), but that psychobiological factors are playing a prominent role in her persistent mutism.

The "squiggle game"

In his therapeutic consultations, D. W. Winnicott made extensive use of a drawing situation that he called the "squiggle game."
This is played by psychiatrist and child. Each takes a turn in ini-
tiating the game by making a "squiggle," that is, a configuration
on a blank sheet of paper, whereupon the other elaborates by adding to it and then telling what it looks like. Gradually, as the squig-
gles become more suggestive and meaningful, they tend to express
the hidden conflict that gives rise to the clinical symptoms. The
psychiatrist uses the drawing game to evoke dream material that
is then interpreted psychoanalytically. As described by Winnicott,
the technique is fruitful in establishing communication with the
child, in loosening the child's defenses, and in exploiting the often
crucial first hour that therapist and child are together.

It comes as no surprise that what starts as a series of "squig-
gles" gradually evolves into animal and human forms.

7

CREATIVITY
AND MENTAL HEALTH

Drawing as a creative activity
Art therapy in psychiatric treatment

Drawing as a creative activity

Children engage in graphic activity with pleasure and enthusiasm. Discovering that they can make something that was not there before, that they can draw a shape at will, that they can with this shape represent something perceived must be a thrilling experience. "To see form emerge in the scribbles of children is to watch one of the miracles of nature" (Arnheim). This vital aspect of children's drawings has been emphasized by Lowenfeld and Brittain and by the present writer. Recently, in studying the creative process, E. De Bono asked young children to design a machine for exercising dogs, something nonexistent. The task was taken up enthusiastically and a fascinating variety of graphic solutions expressed interesting if impracticable ideas.

The adult is well advised to admire and encourage graphic activity but to stand aside and allow the child to discover for himself that he has created an image. This chance discovery is the first step and a basic one in the development of artistic and scientific creativity. What is at issue here is the awareness that perception and reaction to the world can be a very personal thing and that the personal approach, free and unfettered, is at the very root of creativity.

The only way the adult can really help is by providing materials and opportunity, encouragement and judicious praise. The materials are an abundance of blank paper and large crayons, pencils and paints being deferred until a greater degree of motor control has been achieved. Questions, guidance, and direction are interference. Coloring books are blocks to creativity. This God-like spark is present in Everyman; its first manifestations are to be hailed, not stifled. Those so gifted will become the artists, sculptors, and designers of tomorrow. Others will channel their creativity into fields better suited to their talents and inclinations.

Art therapy in psychiatric treatment

The significance and value of graphic expression in the diagnosis and treatment of emotional disorders is being increasingly recognized. The art therapist can help in uncovering and in healing deeply implanted disturbing material that resists verbal expression. But apart from its value as a means of tapping the unconscious, the very act of creating may play a role in prevention and in healing.

In releasing creative energies, many experience, perhaps for the first time in their lives, a personal satisfaction that may be emotionally stabilizing and ego supportive. In this process, the role of sublimation is effective in deflecting potentially disruptive impulses into creative outlets.

Encouraging creative expression, especially in the young, is more essential today than ever before. Many forces in our world tend to stifle the child's need for self-expression through creative endeavor. The passivity of long hours of television, the mechanisms for the production of mindless instant art, and the stress on acquisition of objects may be singled out as particularly inimical to creativity. These things are not making children happy. Mental stability is threatened as youth must choose whether to conform, reform, drop out, or destroy.

The introduction of art therapy into psychiatric treatment services has been slow and difficult. Scepticism and misunderstanding account for much of the indifference and resistance to a technique that has proven itself helpful to many emotionally disturbed patients. This is due partly to the lack of clarity in just what is intended by art therapy. So much depends upon the aptitude, sensitivity, and experience of the individual therapist. Two different approaches are represented by two highly skilled practitioners, E. M. Lyddiatt in England and E. Kramer in the USA.

Lyddiatt bases her procedures on the teachings of C. G. Jung that we all need to become aware of our "individual" and "collective" unconscious. Through spontaneous "imaginative activity" the patient actually treats himself by giving form to his imagination through painting and modeling. In the process, unconscious material is brought to the surface and given graphic expression. This is the crux of the healing process: the disturbing unknown becomes known as a link is established between the unconscious and the conscious mind.

Kramer's procedure differs in that it strives to stimulate and encourage creative activity not as a means of uncovering deeply hidden unconscious material but for the healing potential inherent in the very act of producing something that confers a sense of satisfaction of accomplishment. Sublimation is recognized as playing a major role as primitive energies are transformed into ego-enhancing achievement, a source of joy to many who are unhappy and ridden with anxiety.

Paradoxically, some gifted artists have produced their best work during periods of intensified mental disorder. At times, the strange drawings by schizophrenic children are strikingly artistic.

PART TWO

Family Drawings

8

THE CHILD

AND HIS FAMILY

The nuclear family
The incomplete family
The extended family

To many of us who have tried to help children with their problems, it has become increasingly clear that the child cannot be viewed in isolation from the family. Regardless of whether it be a biological, surrogate, or artificial family, or even a fantasy, it is for the child a transcendent reality that profoundly affects self-image and interaction with the environment of persons and things.

The family forms the earliest and most persistent influence in the life of infant and young child. In discussing the impact of family, T. Lidz writes that "subsequent influences will modify those of the family, but they can never undo or fully reshape these early core experiences." And in an excellent study of children without families, A. Freud and D. Burlingham have observed how in children living in residential nurseries emotions that would normally be directed towards parents "remain undeveloped and unsatisfied, but . . . latent in the child and ready to leap into action the moment the slightest opportunity for attachment is offered . . . "

I venture to say that most psychiatrists would agree that the family is the most fruitful place in which to search for the causes of behavior disorders.

As the child grows older, interest and feelings are extended to include people outside the family circle. Outside factors become increasingly influential in shaping attitudes and behavior, but the family or the lack of it continues to be the basic, most determining influence because it was there that the child learned or should have learned how to deal with his own and other people's feelings.

The nuclear family

me   mother   father   puppy

FIGURE 66

The incomplete family

FIGURE 67

Family as drawn by a girl of 7 years 8 months living with mother in a fatherless home. The child is timid, over-protected, lacking in self-esteem, requiring repeated reassurance, intelligent but doing poorly at school. The mother is tense, anxious. The drawing represents mother (the slightly larger of the two) and the child herself. The tiny figures are without hands.

The extended family

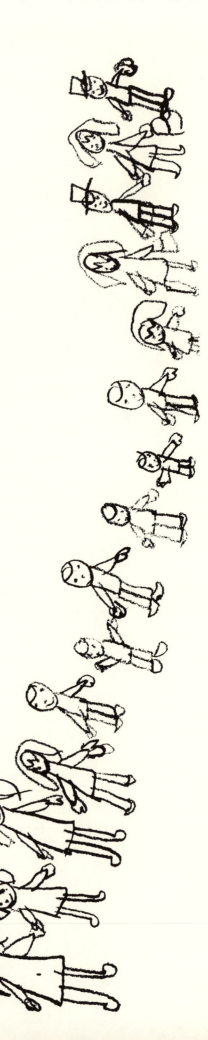

FIGURE 68

Drawn by a Puerto Rican girl of 9 years 4 months. She had been asked to draw a picture of her family.

9

"DRAW YOUR FAMILY"

The cognitive/affective ratio
The family drawing as a projective technique

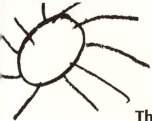

The cognitive/affective ratio

Children's drawings of the family are valuable expressions of their feelings and how they view the transactional patterns within the family. There is a substantial difference between the Draw-a-Person Test and the drawing of the family. The first is scored quantitatively, the second is primarily qualitative.

The Draw-a-Person Test has been widely accepted as a measure of intellectual maturity and constitutes an essential component of the psychologist's battery. But while the drawing of a single human figure can be shown to correlate substantially with well-standardized tests of intellectual ability, the same cannot be said for the human figure drawn as part of a family group.

Having repeatedly observed this disparity, I have come to regard it as a shift in the cognitive/affective ratio. When asked to draw a person, most children will respond by drawing their concept of the body image, a predominantly cognitive response. But when asked to draw their family, the response will tend to be colored by affective elements, hence the frequently noted inferior product if one of the figures is rated quantitatively by the Goodenough-Harris method. It is precisely this mobilization of feelings that, while rendering the family drawing less valuable as an indicator of intelligence, confers upon it significance as an expression of the child's emotional life. The family drawing, then, can be viewed as an unstructured projective technique that may reveal the child's feelings in relation to those whom he regards as most important and whose formative influence is most powerful.

FIGURE 69

In **Figures 69 and 70,** drawn by a 12-year-old girl, note the higher level of intellectual maturity expressed in the drawing of a single figure as compared with that of the figures in the family drawing. Although the two drawings are presented here to show the shift in the cognitive/affective ratio when the child draws the family, there are other noteworthy features. The single figure, which she called a lady, has teeth and large arms and hands, besides being ornately dressed with fancy hairdo and wristwatch. And the sun is shining.

The family drawing depicts from left to right, a cousin, another cousin, their father, the child's sister, and the child herself. It is raining and there is a cloud in the sky. She has omitted her parents and has drawn herself last and helpless without arms.

FIGURE 70

The same discrepancy between lone figure and family drawing is evident in **Figures 71 to 73,** drawn by a boy of 8 years 7 months. He was adopted but was not told until he was 8. The single figures represent a "Martian." In drawing his family, the figures are diminutive, resting at the lower margin of the page, and decidedly simpler in execution, again showing the shift in cognitive/affective ratio.

FIGURE 71

FIGURE 72

103

FIGURE 73

The family drawing as a projective technique

As a projective technique, family drawings are especially revealing during the child's latency period, roughly between six and ten years, when graphic expressions are still relatively free from the cultural pressures that tend to make them a more conforming, less individual statement.

Asked to draw the family, most children will cooperate unhesitatingly. Younger children will draw each member standing full-face and separated from the next, all members lined up in a single row or in two levels, like the saints along a medieval cathedral portico. Importance will be expressed by size and location, with the lowliest at the end of a row or even omitted. Affinity may be indicated by proximity or similarity of attire; rejection, by relegation to the end, elimination, or, as in one instance, by representing the sibling as a worm. Expression of feelings may be explicit, but is more typically symbolic.

Older school-age children will be able to portray movement, usually after the original full-face orientation has shifted to profile. The examiner may then ask the child to draw the family in action, each member doing something. The result may display pleasant or hostile interaction—or no interaction at all, with each member doing something in isolation. Common appurtenances of everyday living are likely to be included with symbolic significance, according to Burns and Kaufman. The reader is referred to their *Kinetic Family Drawings*, which treats of the diagnostic and therapeutic use of these action drawings.

At younger age levels, my direction is simply, "Draw a picture of your family." Who shall be included or omitted is entirely and most significantly up to the child alone; the vast majority of children will include all members, often the dog or cat as well. I never tell the child to include himself in the family picture. Were I to do so, I would forego one of its most revealing aspects: how he sees himself in relation to those who count most in his life, if at all. The examiner does not manipulate the situation but simply offers the materials and functions only as observer and recorder while the child is drawing.

Even when dealing with a child old enough to portray movement, I first request that he draw the family before having him draw everyone including himself doing something. I consider it essential to ascertain first if and how the child sees himself in the family group. Having obtained that drawing, I will ask for a kinetic family drawing according to the procedure described by Burns and Kaufman, instructing the child to include himself.

What can the family drawings tell about the child's feelings towards his family, about his status, his fears and uncertainties, his self-image? Can they help uncover the excessive anxiety that is corroding his self-esteem and interfering with the free exercise of his intelligence?

Among younger children, the Draw-a-Person Test and especially the "Draw Your Family" test are probably the most valuable of the projective techniques in that they are not dependent upon the child's willingness or ability to give verbal expression to his emotional conflict. In the family drawing, one may see how the child feels himself to stand in relation to those who count most in his life.

Those of us who recognize the value of these unconscious expressions of feelings do not believe that we are overstating the case in saying that they are more revealing, certainly more lasting, than words. What are some of the indicators of maladjustment?

Taking into account the child's age, intelligence, and maturity how do the family drawings reveal the child's reaction to emotional conflict: anxiety, depression, hostility, self-effacement, withdrawal?

This discussion is centered on family drawings since these, for reasons already mentioned, are more likely than lone figure drawings to reveal affective elements and attitudes.

10

INDICATORS OF

FAMILY RELATIONSHIPS

Omission of a family member
Omission of self
Relative position
Similarity
Relative size
Effect of divorce
Role in the family
Interaction and isolation

Omission of a family member

"Forgetting" to include a family member is expresssive of a negative attitude towards that person, rejection or symbolic elimination.

FIGURE 74

A boy of 8 years 6 months. Presenting problem: destructive, defiant, restless and disruptive at school (D in conduct), frequent lying. He has drawn father first, then his stepmother, and himself. He has omitted his 5-month-old half-sister, born of his father's remarriage. He does not consider this baby as part of the family. He often expresses fear that the baby will die every time she has a cold (wishful thinking).

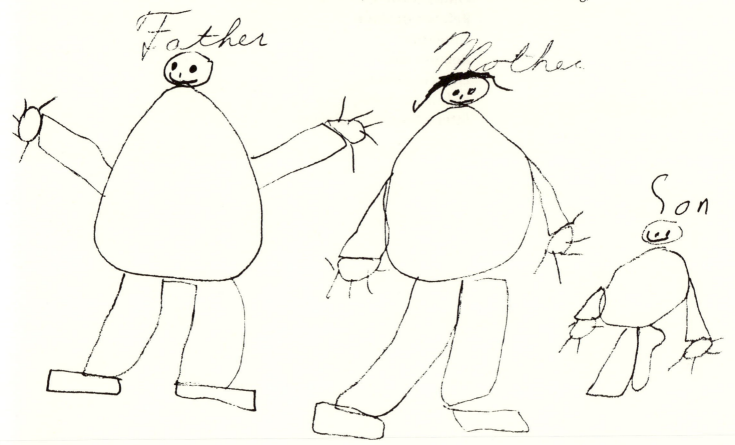

Omission of self

It is unusual for a child to draw the family and not to include all members. Omission of self is seen in drawings by children with feelings of inadequacy or of not belonging. Parental dissatisfaction, excessive criticism, unfavorable comparison with siblings tend to foster low self-esteem and to stifle initiative and the will to achieve.

In a less explicit display of the same problem, the child may relegate himself to the very end of the series of family members, not through modesty but as an expression of low status. This is more significant when all others are in chronological order and the child is not the youngest.

FIGURE 75

An 11-year-old boy of average intelligence, who exasperates his parents by endless dawdling over homework and periods of enuresis, has drawn this picture of his family. He has omitted himself. He is being continually scolded and punished, and is telling in this drawing that he feels he doesn't belong.

FIGURE 76

A girl of 12 years 10 months has drawn her family. Everybody's happy, arms around each other, but she is not among them. She is a bright child, who will not sleep alone because she has a fear of death.

Father

Mother

Aunt

Uncle

Grandmother

FIGURE 77

Drawn by a 10-year-old boy. He is of average intelligence but reads poorly. Manifests feelings of inadequacy and low self-esteem. Insecure. He has drawn himself last. He expressed a wish to be closer to his father. There are dark clouds overhead.

Relative position

The child will tend to place himself next to the favored parent or sibling.

FIGURE 78

Drawn by a boy of 9. In his drawing of his family two of the figures are in profile. He has not quite mastered this orientation so one of the profile figures has two eyes shown. The boy has a good relationship with John and has placed himself next to him. The figures are not in chronological order.

mom

Helen

John   KEVIN

Pam

Dad

mike   patty

Similarity

Affinity may be indicated by distinctive clothing, different from that of other family members but similar only to that of one of the family, usually a sibling, with whom the child is in good rapport.

FIGURE 79

Drawn by a boy of 9. Average IQ. Poor school work. Unmotivated. Feelings of inadequacy. Insecure. He has drawn his family beginning with father and mother, then all the children in descending order of age from his 18-year-old brother down to a 5-year-old brother. He is the fourth from the right, in proper age order. He has a strong attachment to his oldest brother. Note that this older boy and the child himself are the only ones with dark shirts.

Relative size

Like the ancient Egyptians, the young child, manifesting what Luquet termed "intellectual realism," uses size to express the importance attributed to a person, the awe and esteem in which that person is held. The family member so large in the drawing (and in the child's mind) may in visual reality be quite small, but to the young child things are what he conceives them to be. "Così è se vi pare" (thank you, Luigi Pirandello, it's quite so with young children: "So it is, if you think so"—but we adults know better, or do we?).

In accordance with the principle of "intellectual realism," domineering women, regardless of physical stature, will be drawn larger than their submissive, ineffectual husbands.

MOTHER

FATHER

SISTER

FRANK

DOG

FIGURE 80

Drawn by a boy of 9 years 3 months. He attained high average scores on both Stanford-Binet and WISC, but his school work is poor. He has school phobia. His 11-year-old sister does quite well at school and is much admired. She is the dominant figure in the family drawing.

Effect of divorce

Divorce tends to affect children adversely at all age levels, but especially so during the early years. Most divorces occur when the children are quite young. The child may be troubled by feelings of guilt, confusion, and general unhappiness with decline in school work and development of negative, hostile attitudes.

Figure 81 is the drawing of a boy of 8, physically well-developed, vigorous, and bright. He has become increasingly belligerent and unmotivated at school. The teacher has complained repeatedly to his mother, who has custody and has recently remarried. The boy visits regularly with his father. An older brother is away at boarding school. The boy will not verbalize his problem.

Asked to draw his family, he has made small figures at the bottom of the page. These figures are arranged in two groups. He has identified the persons from left to right as his mother and her husband forming the first group, a space, and then a second group comprising the boy himself, his brother, his natural father, and the dog. Although living with his mother and her husband, the boy has elected to include himself in the group with his father. It is reasonable to assume from these facts that he has indicated where he feels he belongs, where he wants to be. Also, the figures are small and standing at the lower margin of the page as though for support. These features have been noted in drawings by insecure children.

The teacher has described the boy as "mad at the world." There is good reason to ascribe his hostility to the parents' separation, divorce, and mother's remarriage. The family drawing is telling us what the boy will not or cannot express verbally. It has facilitated understanding of the boy's misbehavior, contributing thereby towards an effective therapeutic approach.

FIGURE 81

FIGURE 82

Family drawing by a boy of 7. His parents separated when he was 4. Does the encompassing figure, which he called "a design," express a wish that his family be reunited?

Role in the family

FIGURE 83

The symbolic significance of arms and hands is interestingly expressed in **Figure 83,** a family drawing by an Eurasian girl of 6 years 9 months. Her mother is Japanese, her father American. The family is composed of the parents and a greatly admired younger brother and herself. She has drawn her family in the following order: her brother (drawn first and unrealistically large), herself, father, and mother. It is noteworthy that only the males have arms. The girl and her mother are clearly distinguishable as females by their hair and dresses. Like her mother, the child is becomingly shy and relatively unassertive but true to the traditional role of the Oriental female. In contrast, her assertive brother, when asked his sex, replied "I'm a BIG boy" though only three.

Interaction and isolation

In drawings by school-age children who are able to depict movement, positive interaction between two members of the family indicates a good relationship or a yearning for a closer relationship, as when a child depicts himself playing ball with father. Hostility may be expressed by the use of weapons or other material directed at the adversary. Lack of interplay among family members is often indicated by depicting each in a separate compartment, doing something alone, in social isolation without reference to any of the others.

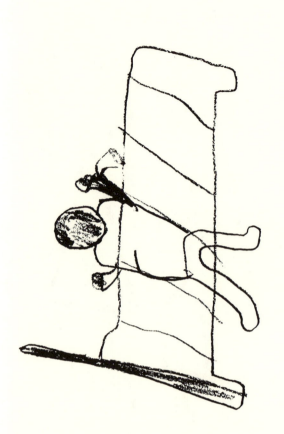

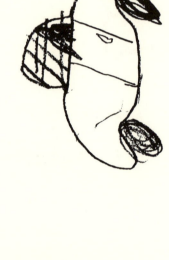

FIGURE 84

A kinetic-family-drawing in which the child depicts members of his family in action, each doing something. Drawn by a boy of 10. The only interaction is between the two figures in the lower left who represent the boy and his father. In real life, father is too busy with work to give enough time to his family. The boy here is expressing a wish for a closer relationship with his father. The other family members are self-contained. The one in the crib is a baby of 9 months.

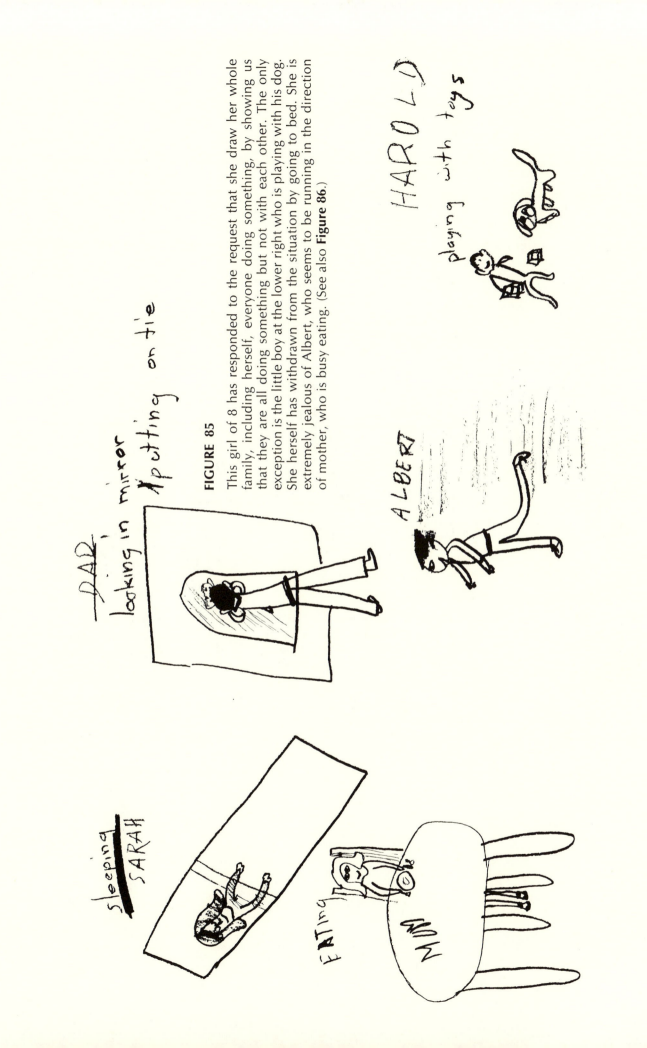

FIGURE 85

This girl of 8 has responded to the request that she draw her whole family, including herself, everyone doing something, by showing us that they are all doing something but not with each other. The only exception is the little boy at the lower right who is playing with his dog. She herself has withdrawn from the situation by going to bed. She is extremely jealous of Albert, who seems to be running in the direction of mother, who is busy eating. (See also **Figure 86**.)

DAD, looking in mirror, putting on tie

HAROLD, playing with toys

ALBERT

sleeping SARAH

EATING MOM

FIGURE 86

This family drawing is by the same 8-year-old girl as **Figure 85.** She is continually resisting and disobeying her mother and just as frequently asking her forgiveness. She is striving for affection and at least for attention. We see her kneeling in a repentant attitude.

11

THE "KNOWING" CHILD

In viewing children's drawings one is at times impressed by the advance information exhibited in matters sexual and reproductive. While most latency children show little interest in these activities other than to scribble some magic word on a wall, children from poor families tend to be uncommonly well aware. They are likely to witness scenes from which most middle-class children are carefully shielded. Restricted living quarters and crowding do not allow privacy. I have also observed similar precocious awareness in children whose parents have divorced and remarried. By and large these are intelligent, perceptive children, not to be confused with disturbed children who may exhibit an inability to set aside a compulsive preoccupation with the sexual organs.

Sex education is highly desirable but children should not share their parents' bedroom.

FIGURE 87

Drawn by a black boy of 7 years. He is currently in foster care. His own home has disintegrated; the children are scattered in various foster homes. He expresses attachment towards the family and vividly recalls each member. He has included them all in this drawing. All have Afro hairdos. The baby he has placed inside mother's body.

FIGURE 88

This girl of 7, of superior intelligence, has clearly portrayed sex differences in body contour and has represented herself as surpassing her mother in femininity.

FIGURE 89

Female figure drawn by a girl of superior intelligence at age 8 years 7 months.

PART THREE

Handicapped Children's Drawings

12

THE INFLUENCE OF
VISION, TOUCH, AND MOTION
ON THE EVOLUTION OF IMAGERY
IN THE CHILD

Vision and touch
Sense and motion

"Only in motility the various impressions of the senses approach the perception world."
Lauretta Bender

"Movement is an essential part of sense perception. He must move his hands to manipulate; just as he must move his eyes to inspect."
Arnold Gesell

Vision and touch

In drawing, the child expresses himself creatively in visual images. These derive from a variety of sensory phenomena, acted upon, assimilated, and conceptualized. The nature of the experiences will affect the form which the image will assume, particularly during the early years, probably the first five, when impressions are vivid, persistent, and often uneffaceable. This view is discussed at length by Piaget and Inhelder in *Mental Imagery in the Child* (1971). Inherent in this hypothesis—that in order to know objects it is necessary to act on them—is the role of motion. But more about this later. For the moment let us concern ourselves with sensory phenomena.

All parts of the eye are fully developed at birth with the exception of the fovea centralis. This minute area of the retina, directly behind the pupil, is destined to become the point of clearest vision, thanks to a growing concentration of retinal cones. This anatomical fact accounts for the inability of the newborn to receive a sharp image on the retina while reacting to light. Anyone who has seen an infant at birth knows how tightly the eyes are shut when a light is flashed into them. At four months of age, a sufficient number of cones has appeared in the fovea to permit the reception of outlines. It is at this time that the infant begins to focus. In conformity with the cephalo-caudad rule of development, the child takes hold with his eyes long before being able to do so with his hands. And yet it is touch and not vision that is the basic sense, the mother of the senses. Indeed, receptive touch antedates birth.

This primacy of touch has been noted by early thinkers. "Every animated body absolutely must have a tactile capacity . . . . Every animal must possess this sense: it does not have to possess another" (Aristotle in *De Anima*). "The sense of touch, the most perfect of all senses, is more perfect in man than in any other being" (Thomas Aquinas).

The intuitions of philosophers have been corroborated by modern men of science as well as by others more directly concerned with the function of that most complex thing in the world—the human brain. It is generally conceded that the reception of sensory material must be processed centrally if it is to have meaning; hence, the traditional distinction between reception of stimuli and their perception. But as far back as 1930, Gesell and Amatruda had written in *Developmental Diagnosis* that the eyes do not function as mere receptors but that like searchlight antennae they are in constant adaptive movement, and that the kinesthetic impressions from their movements are as essential as the retinal impressions for an awareness of the configuration of objects.

More recently, R. Arnheim has expressed firm opposition to the generally held view that the senses receive and the intellect learns to interpret. He rejects the dualism that would have the senses simply gather perceptual material, while the higher cognitive levels convert it into concepts. In asserting the active selectivity of vision, Arnheim includes the activity of the senses, and particularly of vision, in the mental operations that are referred to as "cognition." The function of the eye is not limited to passive reception. Leonardo went even beyond in affirming that the eye not only takes in but actually sends forth stimuli. I am not able to say whether it is true that the ostrich and spider are able to hatch their eggs by simply staring at them, but I am inclined to agree that maidens "have the power in their eyes to attract the love of men."

Though vision and hearing are destined to become the most comprehensive and efficient reporters of what goes on in the world outside, there can be little doubt that touch is the medium of our first impressions. The rooting reflex may serve to illustrate the primacy of the tactile sense. This reflex enables the newborn to turn his head and draw into his mouth the nipple as soon as it touches his cheek. It is only later, at four months, that he excites and purses his lips at the mere sight of the wanted breast or bottle. Through touch, he has learned to see. An unconditioned reflex has become a conditioned response.

The tactile sense is the one most widely distributed. Receptors for touch, heat, cold, and pain are found in all parts of the skin, which, by the way, is the largest organ system in the body. Information is also conveyed to the brain from muscles and joints. A concentration of sensory receptors in mouth and fingers is reflected in the large area by which these structures are represented in the sensory cortex of the brain. It is through the mouth that the newborn makes a first significant contact with the world, with his mother's body. Deprived of sight and hearing, Laura Bridgman and Helen Keller were able to communicate with the outside at the highest level entirely through the skin. But without touch, the mind cannot grow because stimuli brought by the other senses have no meaning.

Beyond its essential role in cognitive development, the tactile sense is the medium by which feeling states are transmitted from mother to infant in an empathetic exchange that will determine to a great degree the personality of the future adult—for better or for worse.

Sense and motion

Sensory phenomena are inextricably and reciprocally interwoven with motion. Vision is motor as well as sensory. The fingers must move in order to feel. Even the imagery of dreams is associated with rapid eye movements. We are accustomed to treating them separately, but even in the cerebral cortex, sensory and motor representation are not entirely segregated. Penfield and Rasmussen have shown that the distinction between motor area and sensory area in the cortex is not clear-cut; that while the primary representation of movement is located in the precentral gyrus, there is a subordinate representation of movement also in the postcentral gyrus. The reverse is also true, that while the postcentral gyrus is the primary sensory area, there is also a representation of sensation in the precentral (motor) area. This finding is of fundamental significance in understanding how and why sensation and movement are intimately and inseparably intertwined.

Perception results from the integration of a variety of sensorimotor experiences. Gradually, the eyes will take over from touch and become the primary receptors, while hearing adds another dimension. By merely looking at a bell, we know that it is hard and smooth and that it rings if shaken. Manipulation, as the term indicates, is a function of hands; but we grasp, as it were, with our eyes what we cannot with our hands.

Fully aware of the artificiality of the dichotomy, a separate discussion of sensory and motor impairments will be adhered to for exigencies of presentation, calling sensory those impairments in which, as in blindness and deafness, the receptive function is predominantly defective as distinguished from those conditions in which the expressive or motor function is primarily defective.

One's concept of the body, the body image, results from the confluence of innumerable sensory and motor experiences and, as P. Schilder has noted, it parallels the child's sensori-motor development. Consequently, sensori-motor impairment will adversely affect the concept of body image and, in turn, its graphic representation.

13

EFFECT OF SENSORY IMPAIRMENT
ON BODY IMAGE

The visually impaired
The hearing impaired
Central language disorders

The visually impaired

Human figure drawings as projections of the body image offer a most valuable device for the study of personality. This technique is obviously inapplicable to the blind child. Clay modeling of the human figure is an appropriate method to assist in developing and in expressing the blind child's concept of body image.

The role of vision is so prominent in perception that its absence cannot but impede the development of an adequate image of the Self and of the world without. It is essential that alternate means be activated early if the child is to acquire a basic self-image from which to perceive the environment with a minimum of distortion. At first, the child must learn to know his body and its parts, and then—in what may be called a dynamic phase—he will have to become aware of his body in space and in relation to other bodies. It is here that movement is an indispensable element. The child perceives his body as an action system. He esteems it for what it is able to do.

This movement aspect in perception is of necessity impaired in the blind child. Every effort should be made to reduce the handicap not only by identification of body parts on self, on others, and on life-size sculpture, but especially by encouraging mobility in the home and outside. He must be helped since he cannot of himself use sight and motion in what Gesell and Amatruda have aptly described as mutual self-correcting combination and reciprocal reinforcement.

The blind should be encouraged to visit museums. Restrictions against touching art objects should be waived in their case. They should be permitted to run their sensitive hands over life-size sculptures so that they too may not only learn but partake of the artistic patrimony of the community of Man.

In her book, *Elizabeth*, Sharon Ulrich tells in vivid detail how she guided her blind baby through the crucial first five years. From early infancy, the world of persons and things was brought to Elizabeth until she was ready to go forth to explore with sensitive fingers the darkness beyond. Of specific relevance to the theme of this chapter are the methods used in promoting the basic concept, that of the body image. The child was encouraged to feel the contours of bodies and to project her own body into space. Like all children, blind children need sex education. The basic difference was first presented by means of a boy doll but that proved unsatisfactory and a real baby boy was volunteered so that the child could explore what other four-year-olds could see.

In the congenitally blind, touch and bodily sensations must continue to be the prime means for the apprehension of form and space. The interpretation of the world outside is essentially subjective and as a consequence the art of those who have never seen will be expressionistic. A degree of realism has been achieved by blind sculptors but this seems to be the result of training.

Reduced vision that is within the limits of usefulness does not seriously impair development of a valid concept of the body image and of the environment. Drawings by myopic, hyperopic, or astigmatic children do not differ substantially from those of their normally-sighted peers. Attempts to account for certain strikingly original, and I might add effective, alterations of subjects by some of the great artists, by invoking some organic defect that causes them to see things unrealistically, may be interesting but most unconvincing. Those who would ascribe the fascinating, highly artistic effects El Greco achieved with his distorted figures to nothing more than an error of refraction, to astigmatism, reveal a mechanistic cast of mind that has difficulty in appreciating, let alone understanding, the transformation of matter into artistic expression. These retrospective diagnosticians do not seem to realize that art and optical reality are not the same. It is not at the site of the retina that the artist formulates his view of the world.

From their studies of visually-impaired children, Gesell and Amatruda concluded that retention of even a small amount of vision could safeguard a child's intellectual development.

After studying a large group, Norris, Spaulding, and Brodie stated that blind children whose need for stimulation and emotional gratification had been adequately satisfied during the crucial early years would be able to adjust well and hold their own in a group with sighted children. Their study confirmed the innate capacity for normal development of blind children who are not brain-damaged. These authors emphasize the importance of encouraging children to make maximum use of residual vision.

One must not overlook the fact that visual disorders are often but one aspect of a more pervasive pathology that involves cerebral areas essential for the reception and processing of information. Many children are multiply handicapped.

The rubella epidemic of '64-'65 has left great numbers of children with residual damage sustained during the early weeks of prenatal development. Impaired hearing, intellectual deficit, defective vision, cardiac malformation—many have one, some have all of these serious handicapping conditions. The behavioral and intellectual consequences have been studied by Chess, Korn, and

Fernandez and are presented in their *Psychiatric Disorders of Children with Congenital Rubella.*

The overall concern in care of the blind child is protection of the personality. The child must learn to achieve maximum mobility and independence. He must be able to go forth into the environment and obtain, without the use of sight, the information that will help him to respond effectively. If the defect is only visual, the problem will be to obtain sufficient data for storage and processing. This can be achieved only by maximum use of auditory and tactile-kinesthetic intake. Effective perception of the outside is achieved by projection of the self into space, hence the necessity to develop an awareness of the body, of its shape, its functions, and its dynamic relation to space and to the persons and things in space. As with the normal child, it is from the body image as a base that the world outside makes any sense.

The visually handicapped child as distinguished from the blind is one who can be taught to use print instead of braille. This child is in a position to develop quite normally—emotionally and intellectually as well as socially—in response to positive parental attitudes and suitable educational modifications. Peculiarities in human figure drawings will reflect intellectual and emotional deviations rather than visual factors.

The hearing impaired

Deprived of hearing, a child learns to intensify awareness of visual cues. Highly alert visually, he will learn to read facial expressions, gestures, and mouth movements, and to communicate his own feelings, wants, and needs by appropriate gesture and pantomime. If sufficient residual hearing is available, amplifying devices will facilitate hearing, listening, and the acquisition of speech. In uncomplicated peripheral hearing loss, intellectual development tends to progress as in the hearing child thanks to progress in special education of the hearing impaired. The threat is to the child's social and emotional life. Impaired ability to communicate verbally is frustrating, often resulting in tantrums, resistance, and rebellion. These behavioral manifestations are not inherent in deafness. They result from misguided attempts to curb symptoms while ignoring the real problem, the child's deafness. Hence, the need for understanding and collaboration between parents and teachers.

FIGURE 90

Spontaneous drawing by a girl of 5 years 7 months. She has a severe sensori-neural hearing loss and, as a consequence, no speech. Note the absence of a mouth. She has drawn nostrils and a navel, large ears, and a disproportionately small body. The figure expresses average intellectual maturity, but the presence of the navel, the diminutive trunk (or exaggerated head size), and the issuance of arms from the head point to immature emotional development.

FIGURE 91

Drawn by a child of 4 years 7 months. Pregnancy was complicated by rubella during the 3rd month of gestation. The child has a sensori-neural hearing loss. No speech. Attends school for the deaf. The human figure expresses a mental age of 4 years 9 months but there is no mouth.

FIGURE 92

Drawn by a girl of 5 years 8 months. She attends a school for the deaf. because of a severe sensori-neural hearing loss. The drawing expresses a mental age of 5 years 9 months, indicating average intelligence. But the figure has no ears.

FIGURE 93

Drawn by a boy, chronological age 6 years 11 months. He attends a school for the deaf because of a sensori-neural hearing loss. He is a secure, outgoing child. Note the large feet, symbolic of a good secure base. The drawing is right in the center of the page, the lines are firm. The drawing expresses fully average intellectual maturity. Like the child himself, the figure is wearing a hearing aid.

Central language disorders

In central language disorders, the difficulty resides in areas of the brain that mediate the highly integrative functions of interpretation of language sounds and their expressive realignment into intelligible speech.

In both types, the peripheral and the central, the end result is the same: failure to develop speech. The mechanism is different —the peripherally impaired does not hear; the other does not understand what he hears.

During the many years that I have been examining young children in a Hearing and Speech Clinic and in a School for the Deaf, I have studied drawings as aids in differentiating the peripherally from the centrally impaired. I have found them most helpful. Since the auditory, language, and educational habilitative program will vary according to the nature of the communication disorder, it is essential to determine whether the difficulty is predominantly peripheral (hypoacusis or sensori-neural hearing loss) or central (developmental aphasia, dysacusis, or central auditory imperception), or combined "central with peripheral."

Differential diagnosis may be quite difficult. A child who hears but who is centrally impaired is either unable to translate speech sounds into meanings (receptive aphasia) or to combine the sounds he hears into the words we use (expressive aphasia). In either case, the child will be unable to communicate verbally. Many such children will turn off what to them is nothing more than an irritating jargon. Failure to respond to sound results not from hearing loss but from failure to understand speech that reaches the brain. Faced with this problem, the diagnostic team will search beyond the threshold-level audiogram into areas of behavior and perceptual functioning.

A child with a peripheral hearing loss but with intact pathways and cerebral speech areas will tend to draw the human figure as do most children who, like himself, are neurologically intact. On the other hand, a child who does not speak because of central language disorder will show signs of cerebral dysfunction commonly seen in drawings by the neurologically impaired, namely, immature concept of body image, perceptuo-motor difficulty manifested by inability to copy geometric forms at a level consonant with IQ as measured by standardized tests.

The examiner will, of course, look for other evidences of cerebral dysfunction. Impaired perception, persistence of concrete thinking, difficulty in controlling attention and motility are common concomitants of central language disorders.

There is a practical need for differentiating between peripheral and central impairment, for upon this determination will depend the emphasis that shall be placed on amplification. In mixed cases, it is important to determine which is the major factor, peripheral or central, in the child's failure to develop speech. In sensori-neural hearing loss, residual hearing will be utilized through amplification; in central impairment, efforts will be directed at overcoming distractibility, improving body image and perception, and building step-by-step a comprehension and utilization of the verbal symbols that constitute our language.

To the solution of the diagnostic problem, children's drawings can make a significant contribution.

FIGURE 94

Central language disorder in a boy age 6 years 10 months. Impulsive. Poor planning of the figure, no room for legs. Fine motor coordination is only fair.

FIGURE 95

Drawn by a girl of 6 years 4 months who has a central language disorder and is getting Ritalin to increase attention span and reduce hyperactivity. She is highly excitable and tends to go out of bounds. This drawing shows poor concept of body image. The figure has only one eye and one leg, no nose, no mouth. It looks more like a chick than a person, but she indicated that it was a self-portrait. The two reversed S's at the upper right are the first letter of her name.

14

EFFECT OF MOTOR IMPAIRMENT ON BODY IMAGE

Motor disability
Organic brain syndrome

Motor disability

Disorders of motion vary in degree and in kind depending upon their intensity, extent, and location in the neuromuscular system. Between the extremes of total disability and mere awkwardness there is a broad spectrum comprising paralysis, involuntary movement, tremor, incoordination, disequilibrium, and weakness. Each disorder may be mild, moderate, or severe; generalized or localized; static or progressive; reflected in disorders of gait, manipulation, or speech.

Without the essential contribution of movement, our perception and response to the world of persons and things would be profoundly and adversely affected. To the degree that a child is limited in ability to reach out, grasp, manipulate, and go forth, relation to the environment will be limited and perception impaired or distorted. Disorder in interpreting sensory phenomena will affect concept of body image and gestalt function. Expressive of the difficulty will be poor human figure drawings and inability to copy geometric forms.

Organic brain syndrome

The original observation of Bender—that children with known organic brain pathology are unable to draw the human figure at a level consonant with their mental age as determined by standardized IQ tests—has been confirmed by other investigators, including the present writer.

If the motor disability is severe, as in spastic tetraplegia in which all four limbs are paralyzed, the usual methods for evaluating intellectual potential and perceptual function are obviously inapplicable. In these cases the Columbia Mental Maturity Test is of value, as it requires only a minimal movement of the head or even a glance to indicate the child's response, his ability to discriminate and to recognize differences and categories. Where disability is less intense or, as in hemiplegia, in which only one side of the body is paralyzed, standard procedures (including drawing tests) may be applied for evaluation. One must bear in mind, however, that in cerebral palsy associated defects are the rule. These may be visual, auditory, perceptual, and intellectual. They will complicate the more obvious disorders of motion. The child will then exhibit the disorders of perception and thinking that we have come to recognize as evidences of "organicity," namely, impaired gestalt function, poor concept of body image, perseveration, and persistence of concrete thinking. The presence of these signs suggests brain pathology even in the absence of conclusive evidence that the brain is not intact. Because of its relevance to learning disabilities, discussion of syndromes of cerebral dysfunction without clearly demonstrable evidence of cerebral pathology will be included in the section on Learning Disabilities.

At this point, specimens of drawings will be presented to show how concept of body image and perceptuo-motor functioning are impaired when the brain has been damaged. In each instance, cerebral pathology is demonstrable and unequivocal.

Figures 96 through 99 are drawn by a child aged 6 years 8 months. Cerebral palsy. Etiology obscure. Abandoned child. Early history unavailable. Spastic tetraplegia. Severe involvement of lower extremities; upper extremities mildly impaired. Speech clear, well developed. Measurable IQ 64 but potential is considered to be greater. Drawings show poor concept of body image and perceptuo-motor difficulty.

FIGURE 96

Draw-a-Person Test. As he drew, the child named the following parts:
head, eyes, hair, leg.

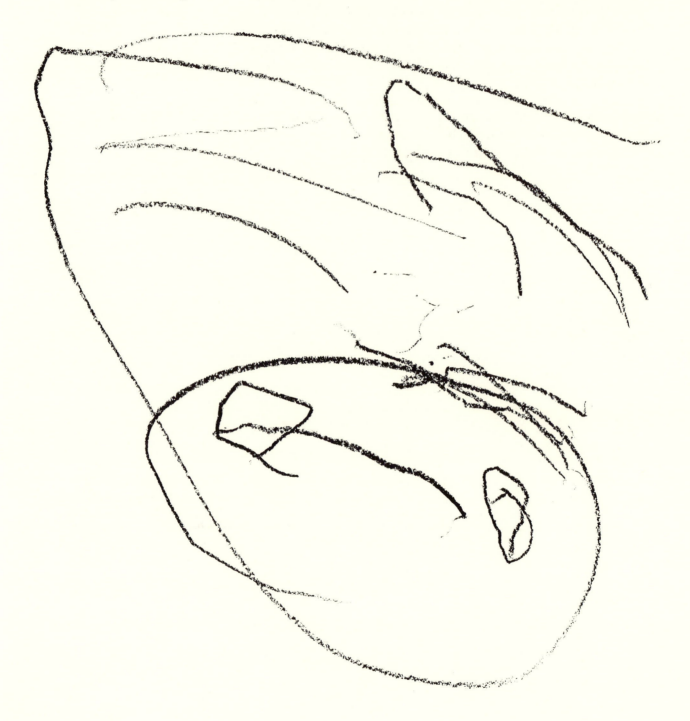

FIGURE 97

Note the 3 strokes in the child's copy of the examiner's cross.

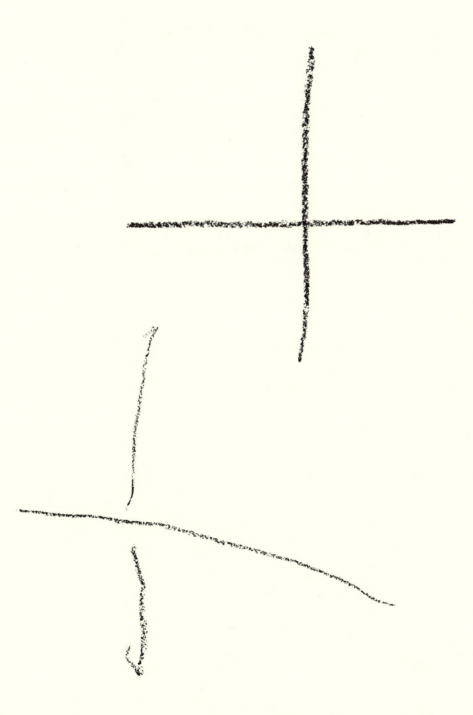

FIGURE 98

Examiner's square and child's copy.

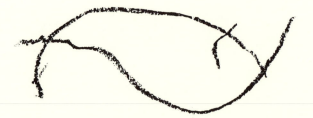

FIGURE 99

Child's second try at copying examiner's square.

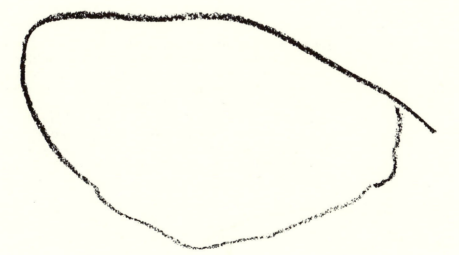

The effect of hydrocephalus on perception was studied by Miller and Sethi on a group of 16 hydrocephalic school-age children. By the ingenious use of Hindi letters and cards with patterns the authors were able to exclude verbal and fine motor influences from the tests. They were thus able to show that in common with other "organic" children, hydrocephalics have great difficulty in the "appreciation of visuo-spatial relationships" and in the ability to "distinguish the key features of a stimulus from irrelevant information within a complex display."

Badell-Ribera, Shulman, and Paddock reported on their study of nonprogressive hydrocephalus in children with spina bifida cystica. Characteristic of their intellectual functioning was a discrepancy between verbal and performance scores on the Wechsler Intelligence Scale. Their relatively high verbal and low performance score is typical of brain-damaged children.

Figures 100 and 101 are drawn by a girl, age 8 years 6 months, in response to the Draw-a-Person Test. This child has a hydrocephalus, treated surgically by pleural shunt. She has a spastic paraplegia. The upper extremities are not involved. WISC: verbal 84, performance 57, full-scale 68 (disparity between verbal and performance IQ). Persistence of concrete thinking: in reply to examiner's question, "What is an orange?" she says, "Something you eat." Poor concept of body image (Goodenough mental age 6 years), distortion of the poorly proportioned figure.

FIGURE 100

"A girl"

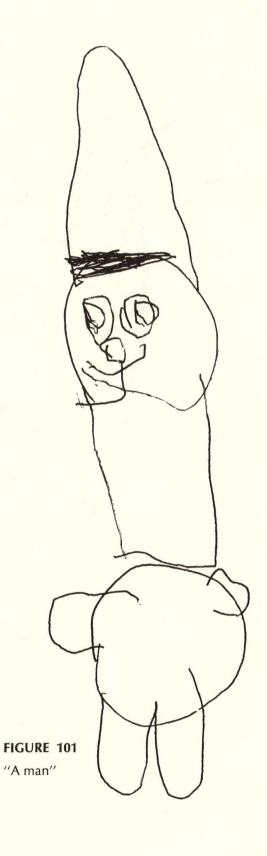

FIGURE 101

"A man"

Figures 102 and 103 are drawn by a girl of 4 years 1 month. Cerebral palsy, mild. Atonic diplegia. Gross motor movements are predominantly involved. Intelligence unimpaired. Concept of body image quantitatively good for her age. Copy of cross is distorted.

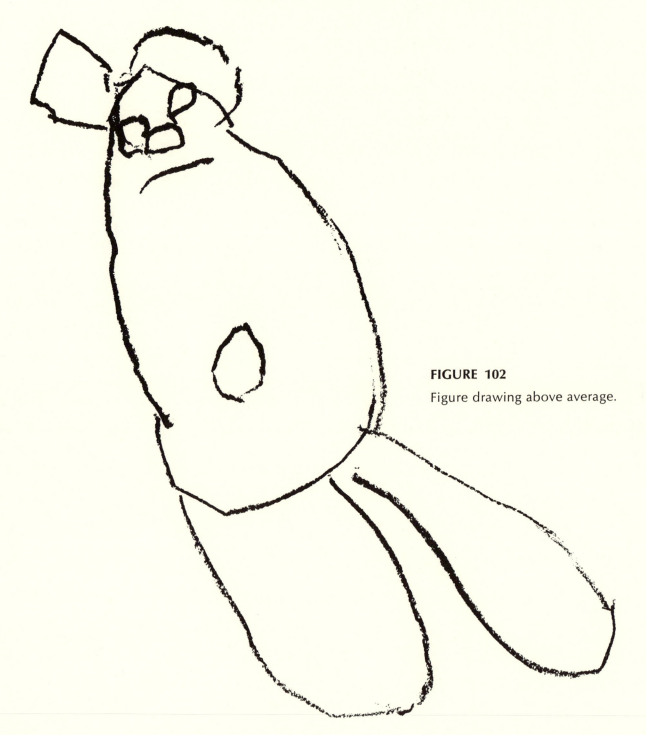

FIGURE 102

Figure drawing above average.

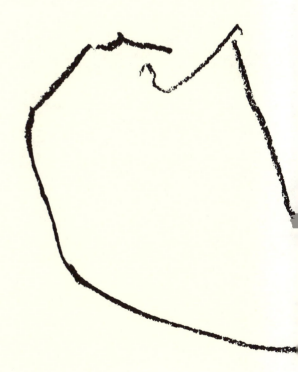

FIGURE 103

Child's copies (right and bottom) of examiner's cross and square.

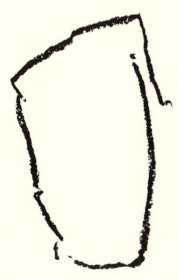

15

HANDICAPPED CHILDREN

Does the drawing indicate the child's disability?

Does the drawing indicate the child's disability?

In reviewing over a hundred drawings by nonverbal children of preschool age, I found only two in which the figure lacked a mouth **(Figures 90 and 91)**.

In a study of drawings by children with impaired hearing, I noted that most of them drew figures without ears or with small ones; but many others drew in ears, so that their figures did not differ in this respect from those by children with normal hearing. Some drew in their hearing aid. Deaf children often omit ears but one must not count on it.

One child with a paralyzed, poorly developed arm drew a figure with one arm smaller than the other, obviously reflecting his own physical deformity.

E. Toker reports on a 7-year-old girl who was to undergo heart surgery for repair of an atrial septal defect. Her drawings show a tree with a hole in the trunk, a projection of the hole in her heart.

More commonly, the handicapped child expresses his defect in more general, less explicit terms, by drawing small figures with tiny or even absent hands and feet. These drawings usually made with small, uncertain strokes express constriction of body image, insecurity, and depression.

In reviewing drawings by obese, compulsive eaters, I have none in which the figure explicitly indicates obesity. In one, interest in food is clearly portrayed. An adopted boy of ten, asked to draw his family, has made them at table having dinner. (The drawing is on page 208 of *Young Children and Their Drawings*). In the present book are reproduced two drawings by the same boy **(Figures 104 and 105)**. Asked to draw a person, he drew a baseball player (an idealized self-image?). When asked to draw a female, he drew one in a shopping center with a cart full of food. The figures are below expectations for a child of his age and intelligence.

In an article on adolescent obesity, Nathan and Pisula direct attention to the poor quality of the laboriously drawn human figures. These authors found disparity between intellectual maturity as expressed by the human figure and that derived from well-standardized IQ tests; and a disparity between verbal and lower performance IQ on the Wechsler Intelligence Scale for Children. The same findings are a feature of drawings by children with cerebral dysfunction.

Also noted by the above-named authors was a relationship between weight gain and increased food imagery in the Rorschach.

The figures drawn do not show obesity. Quite the contrary, they are more likely to express the wished-for rather than the real body.

A study by Green and Levitt of 25 children with congenital heart disease indicated that they tend to draw themselves smaller than do their normal peers. While many are indeed smaller, the graphic projection of the self as small is interpreted as a constricted view of their bodies.

Returning to the question under consideration, whether children specifically portray a physical deviation, my answer is an affirmative qualified by "sometimes." When it does occur, its meaning is strikingly clear. But more typically, graphic expression of impairment is more diffusely represented by a small, hesitantly drawn figure with small hands and feet that tell feelings of inadequacy and need for support.

FIGURE 104

FIGURE 105

PART FOUR

Learning Disability

What is meant by "learning disability"?

In reality, any child who is unable to learn to speak, write, read, or acquire mathematical concepts, whatever the reason, is learning-disabled. Usage, however, has restricted application of the term to those children whose difficulty is not due to mental retardation, sensory deficit, or environmental deprivation.

My selection from among many definitions is the one proposed by the Council on Exceptional Children: "A child with learning disabilities is one with adequate mental abilities, sensory processes and emotional stability who has a limited number of specific deficits in perceptive, integrative, or expressive processes which severely impair learning efficiency. This includes children who have central nervous system dysfunction which is expressed primarily in impaired learning efficiency."

16

VALUE OF DRAWINGS
IN EARLY DETECTION
OF LEARNING DISORDERS

Perceptual impairment
"Minimal brain dysfunction"
Drawings reveal perceptuo-motor impairment
Perseveration

Perceptual impairment

What is perceptual impairment? One's answer will vary according to one's concept of perception.

For practical purposes, Forgus has defined perception as a process of information extraction involving sensory reception, decoding, association with previously experienced and stored input, personality, and motivation. Together, these elements of the process will determine the encoded response.

Piaget has emphasized the learning aspect: we learn to see. The perceptual material must be acted upon before it can become known.

Gestalt psychologists have stressed an innate capacity to organize perceptual material.

If one considers perception as the interpretation of input, then one cannot properly speak of perception without prior experience. This view, however, does not rule out the existence of an innate ability to discriminate form.

Studies on animals and on human infants by Fantz indicate that there is an interaction between innate neurological and maturational as well as learning factors in the development of perceptual functions.

Arnheim rejects the commonly held view that the senses gather perceptual material and that the higher cognitive functions convert it into concepts. He emphasizes the active selectivity of vision as inseparable from perception and cognition, expressing this unity by the term "visual thinking."

In light of the theoretical explanations and experimental data mentioned, perceptual impairment might be defined as a defect in one or more of the steps involved in extracting information from sensory raw material. The reciprocal interaction between sense and motion in perception accounts for increasing use of the term "perceptuo-motor" as more accurately expressing the process.

In line with Piaget's hypothesis that perception does not reach beyond the level of preoperational thought, that perception must be subjected to mental operation in order to be assimilated as knowledge, it follows that defectively perceived material needs to be corrected by mental operation. Unless this occurs, defective information can only result in defective knowledge. According to Piaget, the child is capable of operational thought at age seven or eight. Before that time, things tend to be taken at face value. The ability to correct misinformation varies with each child, intelligence being a prime factor.

Unless there are emotional reasons for the child's academic difficulties, failure to learn in a child of average or superior intelligence is very likely due to impairment at the perceptuo-motor (preoperational) level. Accordingly, I shall offer examples of drawings by children who are of average IQ but who have difficulty in learning to read and write.

"Minimal brain dysfunction"

Cerebral dysfunction may be objectively demonstrable or it may be assumed from symptomatology that is typically observed in patients with known and demonstrable brain damage through injury or disease.

"Minimal brain dysfunction" is a term applied to a questionable entity in which objective incontrovertible evidence of brain pathology is lacking. The neurological investigation, including X-ray studies and electroencephalogram, fails to reveal any other than equivocal or borderline deviations from the normal. In these cases, despite behavioral evidence of dysfunction, it is unwise to use the terms "brain-damaged" or "brain-injured." Voices have been raised against the more appropriate term "minimal brain dysfunction" on the grounds that there is no proof that the brain is the seat of the disorder.

Those of us who have dealt with this problem know how painful it can be to be told that something is wrong with a child's brain. To many parents this judgment implies that the situation is irremediable and hopeless. Of course, one has to give some name to the symptom complex, a syndrome usually manifested by aimless activity, short attention span, perceptuo-motor difficulty, awkwardness, persistence of concrete thinking, perseveration. While the child seems merrily engaged in his ceaseless, fruitless, graceless movement, his behavior is most wearing on the parent. It is especially disturbing when the parent discovers that the child is disruptive at school and unable to learn because of inability to attend.

It is not without good reason that many object to labeling the child instead of helping him to overcome the disability, which can be done without a label. There are ways in which perceptuo-motor dysfunction, defective concept of body image, and other deficits can be overcome. Perceptual training programs, such as the Frostig method, are proving helpful in this regard. Designating them as "children in need of perceptual training" or whatever it is that they need, would be, it seems to me, a more practical as well as a more positive way of looking at the problem—certainly less threatening to those parents who are disheartened by diagnosis of cerebral damage with its connotation of irreversibility and finality. It is not always prudent to call a spade a spade, especially when it may not be one.

Drawings reveal perceptuo-motor impairment

Remedial measures are most effective when applied early. Early, accurate detection of an impending problem provides the opportunity for effective prevention.

Drawings can be most helpful in revealing the perceptuo-motor impairment that foreshadows difficulty in the key areas of writing and reading. Underlying these achievements is the ability to recognize and to use the symbols of our language. These may differ slightly in form but greatly in significance. A child who is perceptually impaired may not notice the differences or may not see them as meaningful.

Examples that follow (**Figures 106-110**) illustrate a boy's difficulty in gestalt function. A 4-year-old boy is unable to imitate a cross though quite able to imitate its component parts when they are presented separately. The cross is demonstrated again, and again he responds with a scribble. To us, and to most children of three, the cross is more than two lines; it is a pattern in which two lines are in a definite relationship, the whole being greater than the sum of its parts. This boy has not perceived it as a pattern.

A follow-up at age 5 years 8 months shows that there is disparity between his intelligence as evaluated by the Stanford-Binet test and his concept of the body image as revealed in his drawing of a person. With an IQ of 92 at age 5 years 8 months, he draws a human figure at a maturity level of 4 years 6 months (**Figure 111**). As is usual with hyperactive, disruptive children, his Social Quotient is low; rated 75 on the Vineland scale. In **Figure 112** he has attempted to print his name (Patrick). In **Figure 113** he has made a fair copy of the square but in **Figure 114** we see that his triangle is poorly drawn and open at the top.

FIGURE 106

Spontaneous drawing at age 4 years.

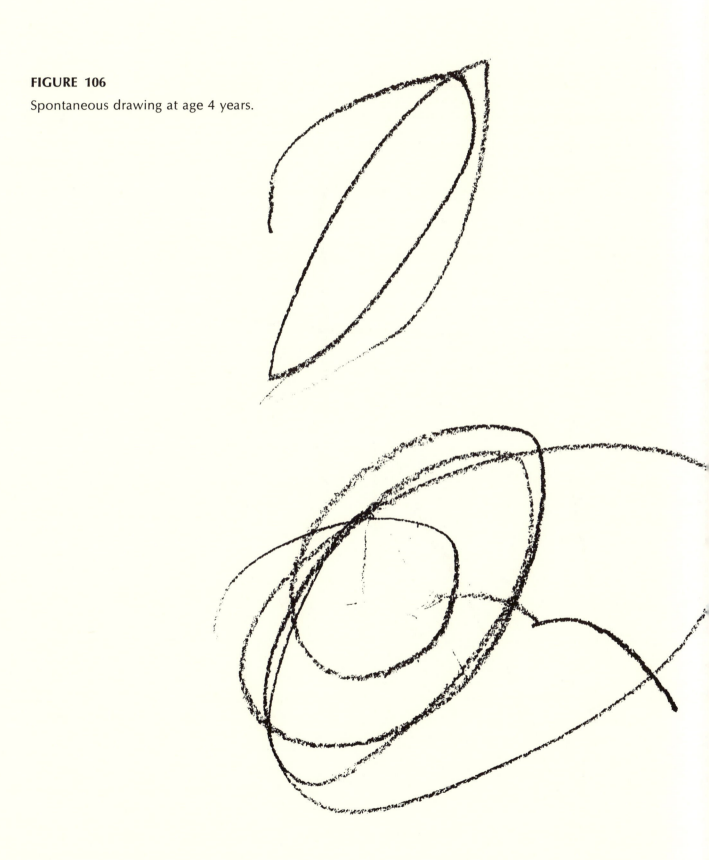

FIGURE 107

Attempt to imitate examiner's cross.

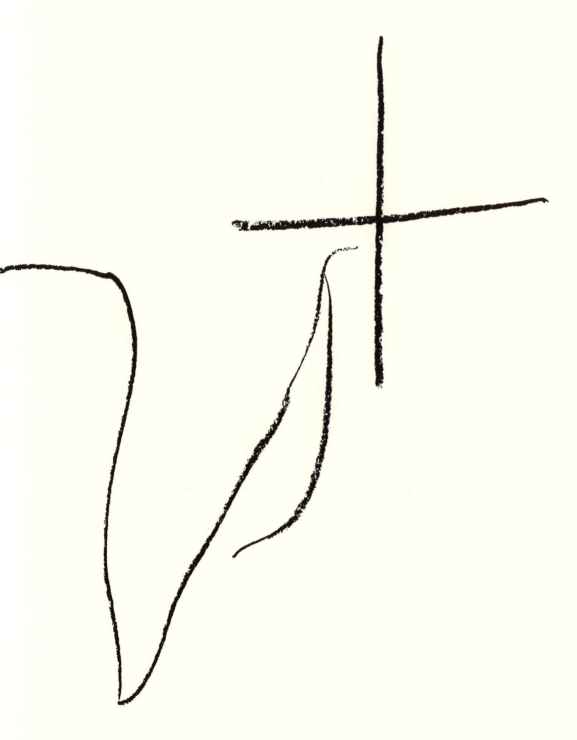

FIGURE 108

Imitates vertical (a component
part of the cross) satisfactorily.

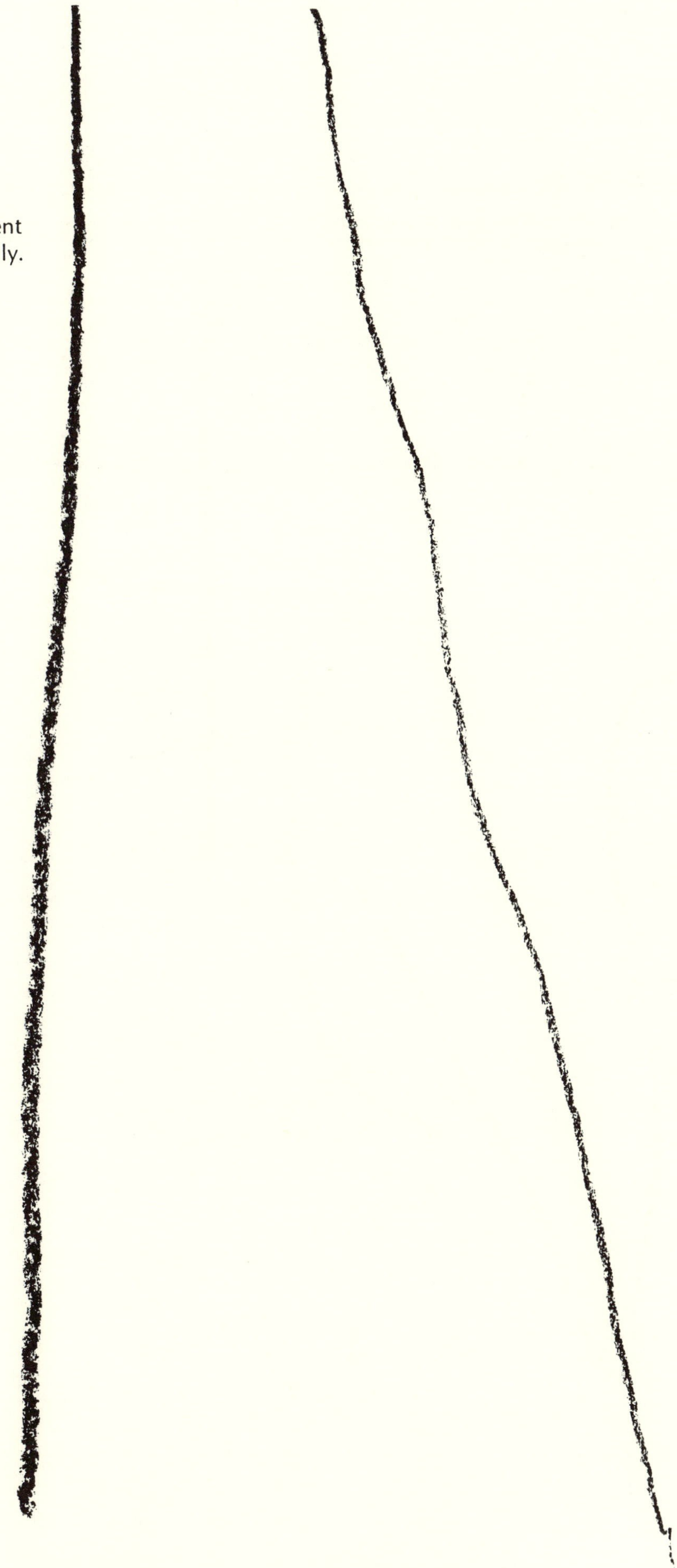

FIGURE 109

Makes a good copy of the examiner's horizontal, the other component of the cross.

FIGURE 110

But this is the result when he is again shown how to draw a cross. He does not perceive the figure as a pattern.

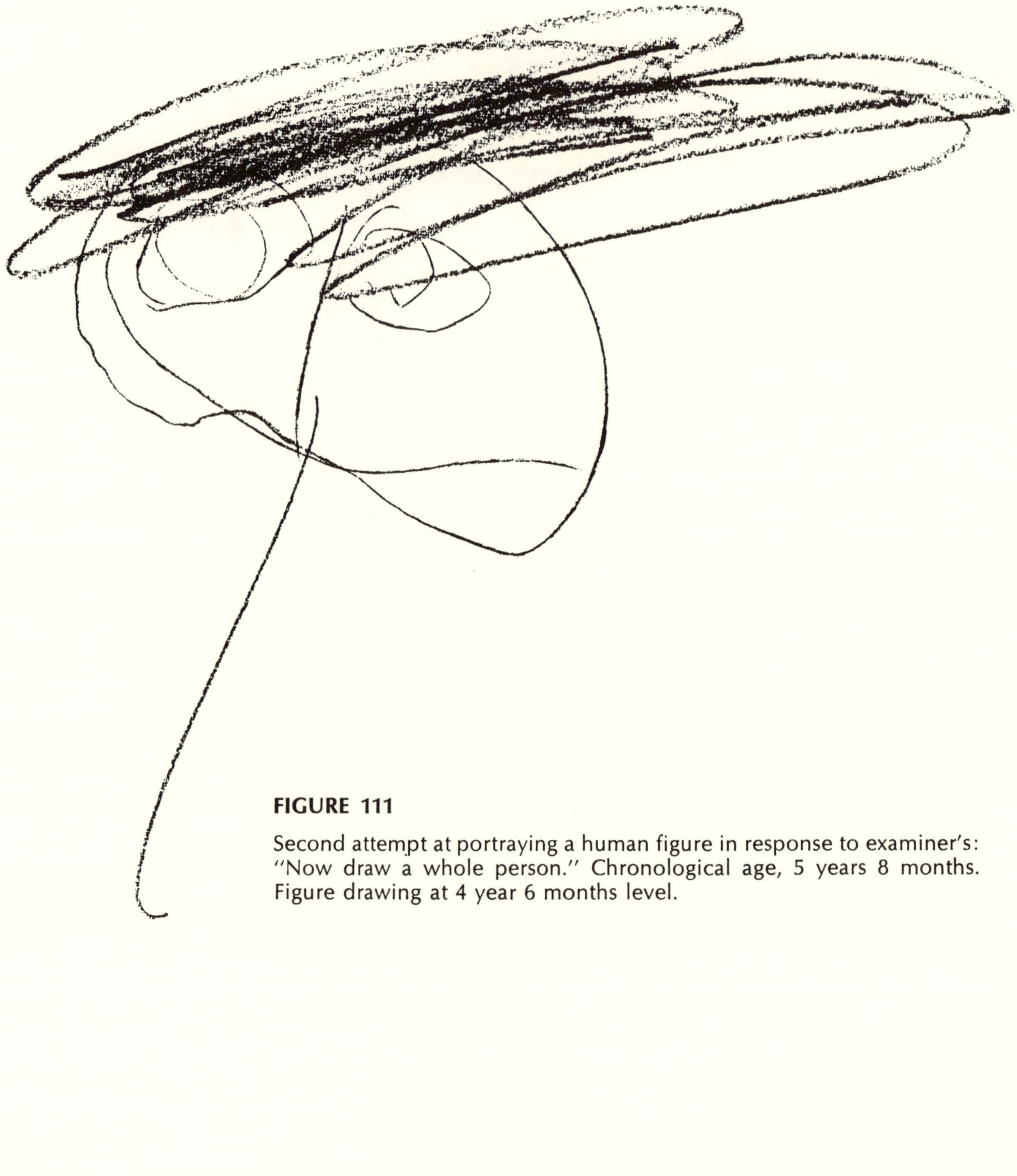

FIGURE 111

Second attempt at portraying a human figure in response to examiner's: "Now draw a whole person." Chronological age, 5 years 8 months. Figure drawing at 4 year 6 months level.

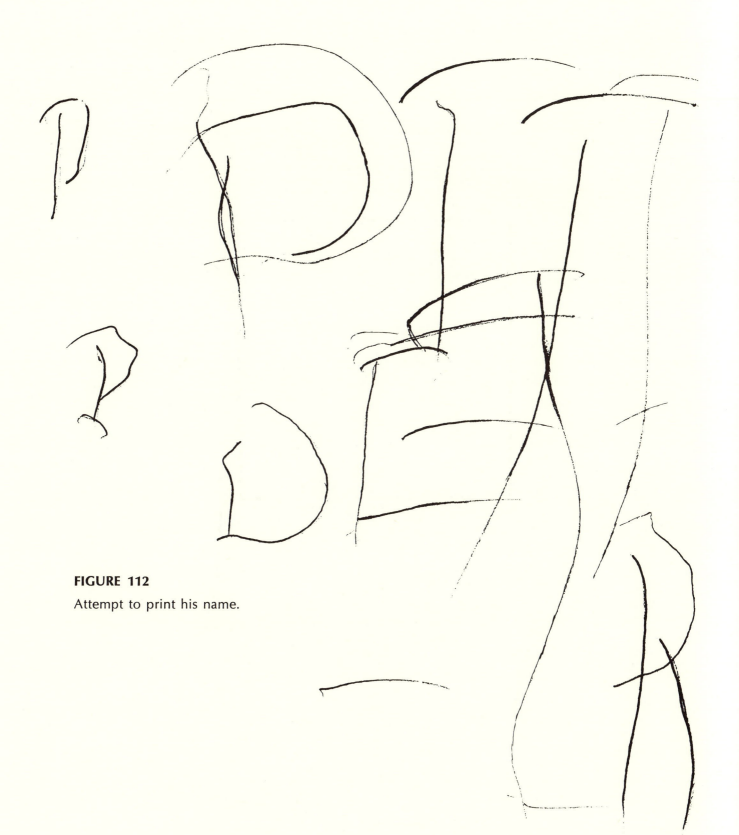

FIGURE 112

Attempt to print his name.

FIGURE 113

Copy of examiner's square.

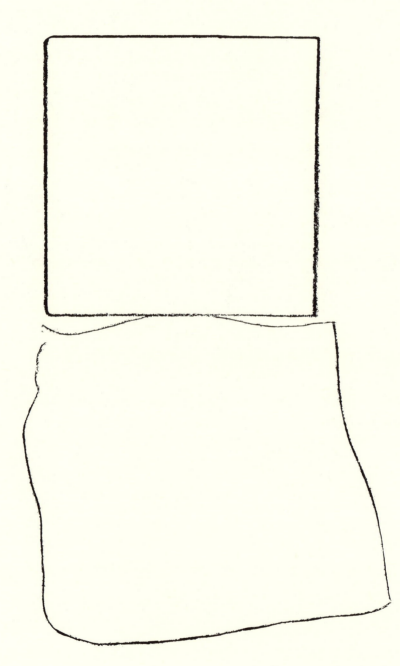

FIGURE 114

Copy of examiner's triangle.

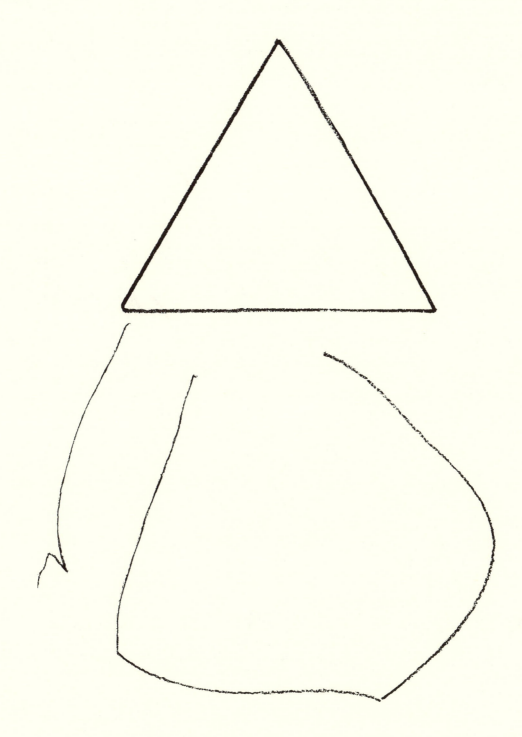

FIGURE 115

Another illustration of the disparity between general intellectual functioning and poor performance in drawing tests, drawn by a girl of 8 years 5 months whose history and clinical manifestations strongly support an impression of brain dysfunction on an organic basis. Results of the Wechsler Intelligence Scale for Children (WISC) were: verbal IQ 91; performance IQ 87; full scale IQ 88. In contrast, her drawing of a person yielded an IQ of 71. Her copies of geometric forms were distorted and rotated.

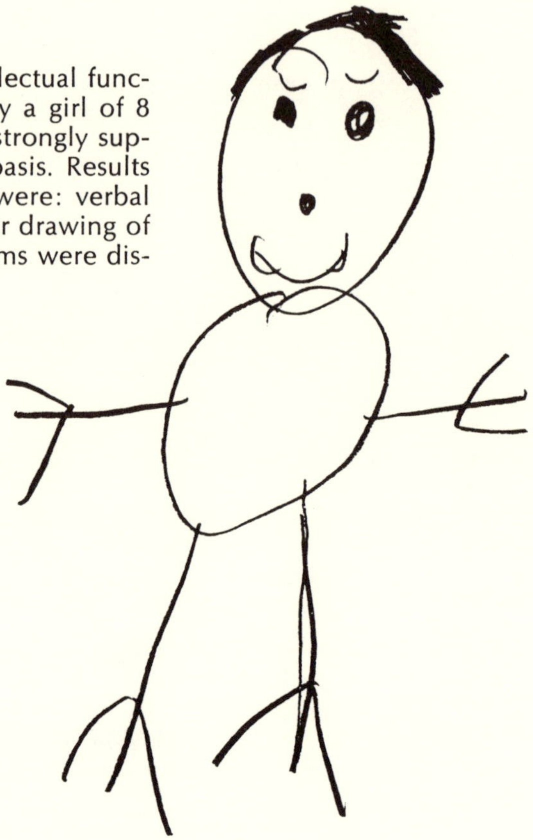

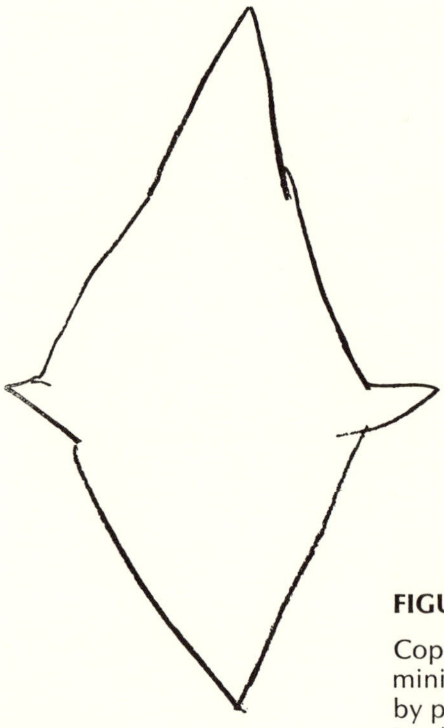

FIGURE 116

Copy of a diamond by a boy of 9 years 10 months, diagnosed as having minimal brain dysfunction. Hyperactive, short attention span, rejected by peers, compensatory overeating (drew his family at dinner). Drawing is characteristic of children with this clinical syndrome, who often render it with "ears."

Perseveration

The tendency to continually and monotonously repeat a demand or an action is a feature of the behavioral complex generally referred to as minimal brain dysfunction. Basic to the problem is the child's difficulty in controlling the attention. Highly distractible, yet unable to disengage his attention once it has been trapped, he tends to repeat the same phrase over and over to the exasperation of his mother, or he may continue doing the same thing long after it ceases to make any sense.

In **Figures 117 and 118** we have two examples of perseveration. In the first, a girl of 12½ has copied the patterns of the Bender Visual Motor Gestalt Test, but instead of limiting herself to the 12 dots on test card No. 1, she goes on to the edge of the page. The same monotonous perseveration is seen in her copy of test card No. 2 on which there are 11 units of three slanting circles. She has made 26 and that is as many as the space will allow.

Figure 118 is the response to the Draw-a-Person Test by a 6-year-old boy of borderline intelligence. His behavior indicates brain dysfunction probably related to Rh incompatibility. Instead of drawing one, he has drawn 12 human figures and they are monotonously alike.

FIGURE 117

Learning disability in 12½-year-old girl. Note perseveration in copying of Bender figures. Perceptuo-motor impairment. Verbal skills highly developed. Difficulty with math. Threatened miscarriage when mother was 7 months pregnant.

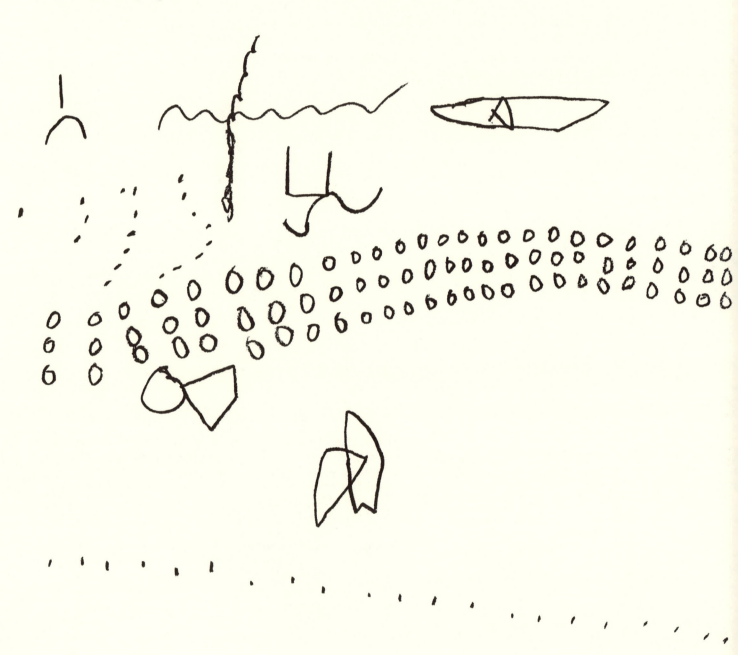

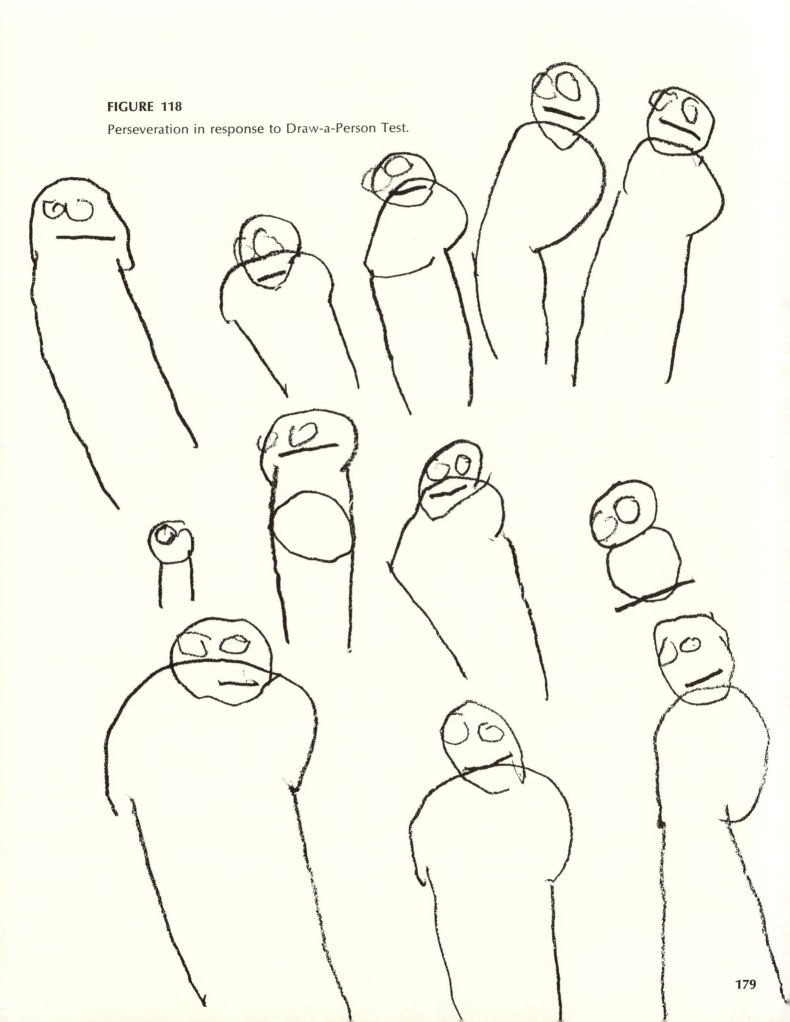

FIGURE 118

Perseveration in response to Draw-a-Person Test.

17

DYSLEXIA

Difficulty in learning to read is a common cause of learning disability and behavior disorders. It affects about 10 percent of American school-age children and is being studied intensively by educators, neurologists, psychologists, and linguists. Its causes have been ascribed to genes, brain dysfunction, visual disorder, perceptual impairment, crossed dominance, poor teaching, cultural deprivation, and to the lack of phonetic consistency of the English language. Among the many attempts to define dyslexia, I have selected that of the neurologist Macdonald Critchley, who characterizes it as "a difficulty in learning to read which is constitutional and often genetically determined, unassociated with general intellectual retardation, primary emotional instability, or gross physiological (including ophthalmologic) defect."

The basic problem is not in seeing but in understanding what is seen. In order to read alphabet languages one must be able to understand the symbols, that is, the letters that make up our words and sentences. The child must be able to attach significance to the small differences in two-dimensional visual symbols that make a "p" different from a "q" and a "b" from a "d," as well as have an awareness of the left to right directional sequences in our language. It is interesting to note that reading difficulty is reported to be rare among Chinese and Japanese school children as they learn a pictographic language. Learning to read is less of a problem in countries that have a phonetic language in which, as in Italian, every letter is pronounced.

Those children who are at risk so far as dyslexia is concerned can be identified before they enter grade school. The child who at four or five exhibits difficulty in recognizing and reproducing simple geometric forms and whose human figure drawings are well below expectation is revealing a need for training in perception, body image, and spatial relationships. Difficulty in right-left orientation and failure to establish lateral dominance are associated signs but not the causes of dyslexia.

Remedial measures should not be delayed until the defects and frustrations of first grade have begun to erode self-esteem and sap motivation.

FIGURE 119

This girl of 5 years 7 months has attempted to reproduce the letters d, b, q, and p. She has drawn a circle and staff, but has failed to alter their orientation. Unless her perception of these markings improves she will not learn to write or read.

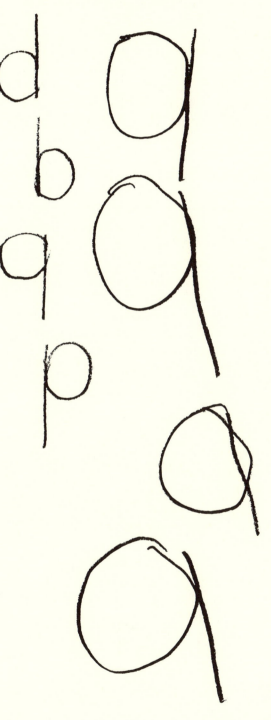

FIGURE 120

Disability in the perception of letters in a 7-year-old girl. This disability can be predicted earlier by a child's inability to reproduce simple geometric designs such as a cross, a square. Early diagnosis provides an opportunity for perceptual training before the child enters the grades.

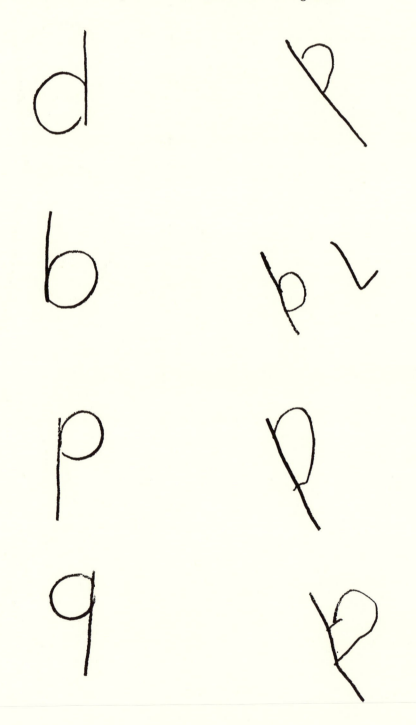

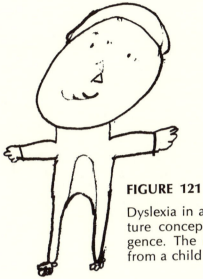

FIGURE 121

Dyslexia in a boy of 10 years 8 months. Immature concept of body image. Average intelligence. The figure is what one would expect from a child of 6½.

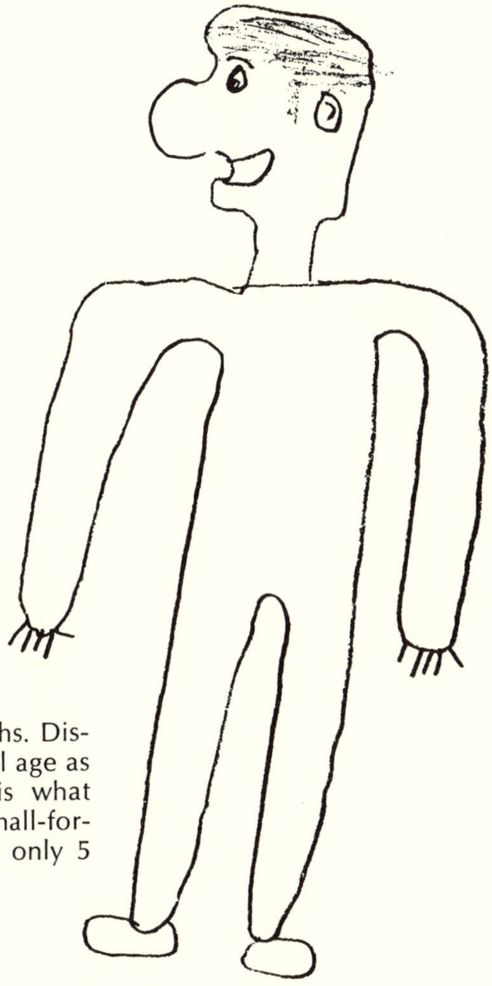

FIGURE 122

Dyslexia in a boy, age 12 years 4 months. Discrepancy between IQ of 105 and mental age as expressed in figure drawing, which is what would be expected of an 8-year-old. Small-for-date baby—born at term, but weighed only 5 lbs. 2 oz.

Figures 123 to 125 are drawn by a boy of 7 years 6 months with dyslexia. Stanford-Binet mental age 6 years 2 months. Reversals. Crossed dominance (right handed, left eyed).

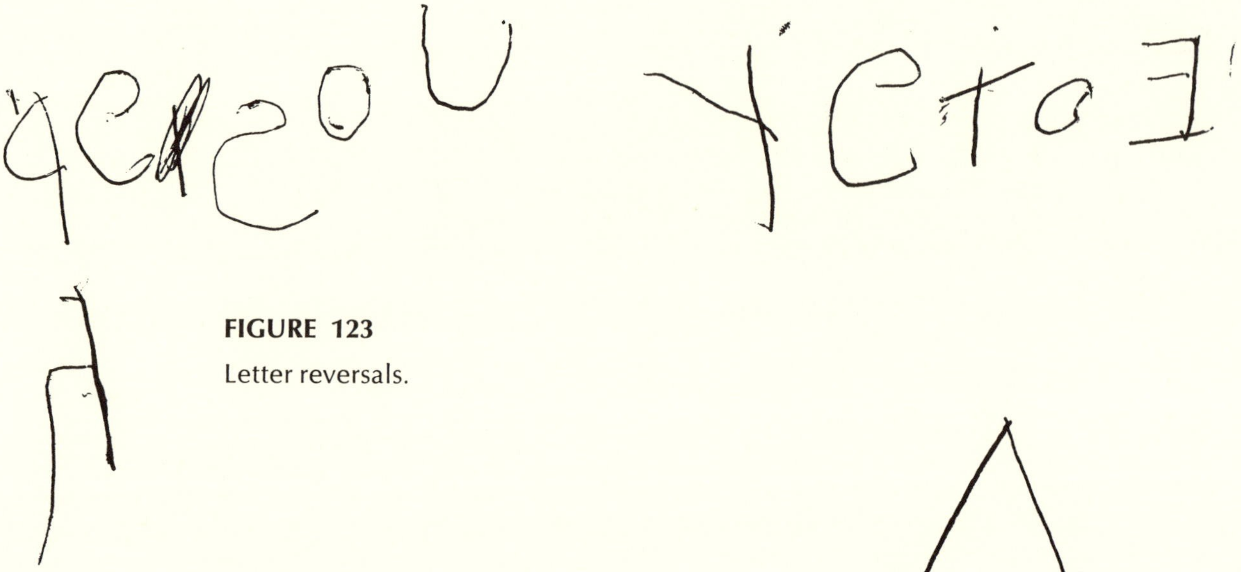

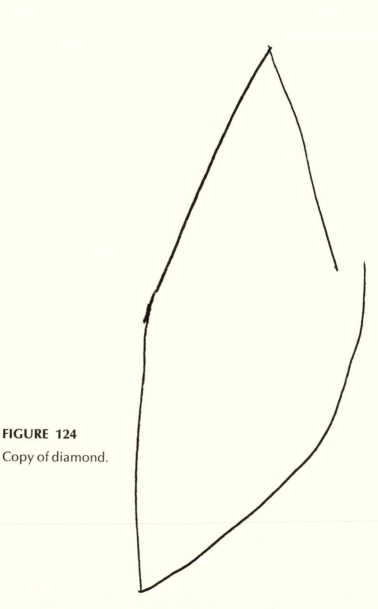

FIGURE 123

Letter reversals.

FIGURE 124

Copy of diamond.

FIGURE 125

Goodenough drawing at 5 year 6 month level. Immature concept of body image.

FIGURE 126

Attempts by a 9-year-old girl to copy diamond.

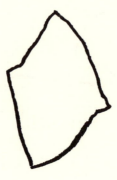

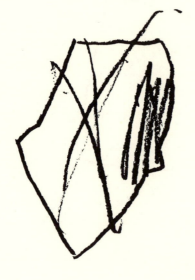

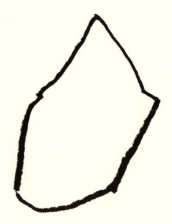

18

DRAWINGS BY CHILDREN
WITH MENTAL RETARDATION

In 1926, F. Goodenough published the first scoring system for the measurement of intelligence from human figure drawings. Ease of administration, its appeal to practically all children, and above all, its validity, have made the test one of the most widely used in psychology. Goodenough used a point score system. In 1963, D. B. Harris published his restandardization of the test. Further refinements in the evaluation of the drawings are suggested in a 1970 publication of the National Center for Health Statistics. The reader is referred to these three classical studies for detailed description of the methods used in establishing norms.

A look at drawings by intellectually limited children will show that a drawing by a ten-year-old with a mental age of five will differ substantially from that by a child of five with mental age of five. The drawing by the retarded child will tend to be disorganized, poorly integrated, and though attaining the same score will often lack some of the more primitive items, while having more mature items not generally included by younger children.

Many mentally retarded children also have serious emotional problems, especially those who, being only mildly retarded, are well aware of their deficiencies. So near . . . and yet so far!

In **Figure 127** a girl of 7 years 5 months functioning in the borderline range has drawn a figure with hands and the correct number of fingers but has omitted the trunk.

Figure 128, drawn by a 6 year 8 month boy with Down's syndrome, is disorganized, unrecognizable. The child called the configurations arms, hair, and legs.

Other examples of omission of more obvious parts of the body while adding pupils to the eyes are seen in **Figures 129 and 130.**

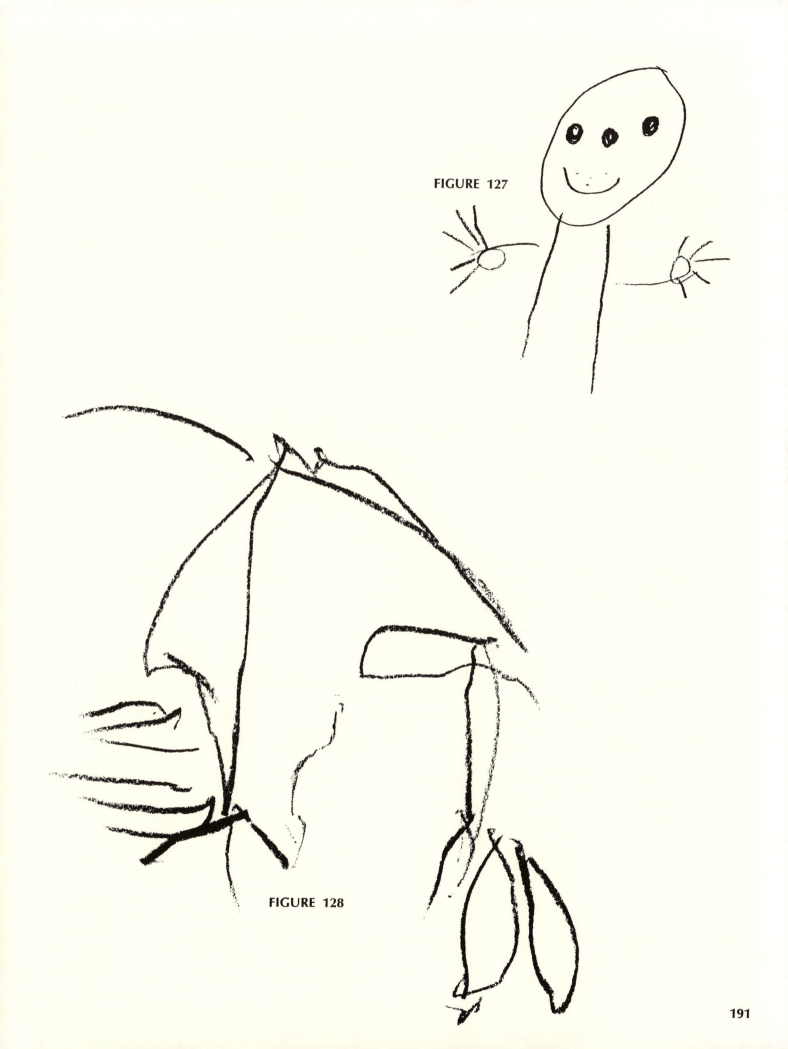

FIGURE 127

FIGURE 128

FIGURE 129

Drawn by an educable child of 7 years 7 months. She has included relatively mature items (hair, pupils, ears) while omitting more basic ones (trunk and arms).

FIGURE 130

It may be impossible to determine from the drawing alone whether it was made by a retarded or an emotionally disturbed child. This "grotesque" figure, typically equivocal, was drawn by an educable retarded child of 7 years 10 months.

19

INBORN ERRORS

OF METABOLISM

Phenylketonuria
Maple syrup urine disease

Phenylketonuria

Phenylketonuria is an inherited disorder of protein metabolism. Both parents, though apparently normal, are heterozygous for the condition; that is, they are carriers. As with all autosomal recessive disorders, the risk figures for each pregnancy are that one out of four children will be affected with the metabolic disorder, commonly known as PKU. These children are unable to metabolize the amino acid phenylalanine because they lack the necessary enzyme phenylalanine hydroxylase. As a result, high levels of phenylalanine are maintained in the child's body. This disorder is associated with mental retardation.

Early diagnosis and the restriction of phenylalanine intake are major factors in the prevention of mental retardation.

For more than ten years, I have had the privilege of cooperating in a long-term study of inborn errors of metabolism by evaluating the behavioral development of affected children. The vast majority of the over one-hundred children in the study have phenylketonuria. The normal functioning of those treated from early infancy stands in strong contrast to the severely retarded development of the older, untreated siblings. The drawings of the children form a permanent record of their progress in response to the special dietary regime aimed at preventing high blood levels of phenylalanine and the associated mental retardation.

Out of many hundreds of drawings, just a sampling has been selected. The first series is by a child in whom early initiation of treatment scrupulously carried out by the parent has produced a good result. In the second child, the result has been poor, for though treatment started early it was not adhered to consistently. Treatment of the third child was begun at age 2 years 5 months; the child was already retarded and the treatment did not reverse the process. But when two years later another child was born to this family, diagnosis of phenylketonuria was made promptly, treatment was started soon after birth, and this child is developing normally.

Phenylketonuria 1

Figures 131 to 133 are examples of drawings by a girl who had special dietary treatment for phenylketonuria starting at age 5 weeks. She is functioning at above average levels at age 5 years 10 months. Her concept of the body image expresses an intellectual maturity of 7 years. Language behavior is also at that level. Her correct copies of the letters d, b, q, and p as well as her copies of geometric figures indicate unimpaired perceptuomotor function. A good result.

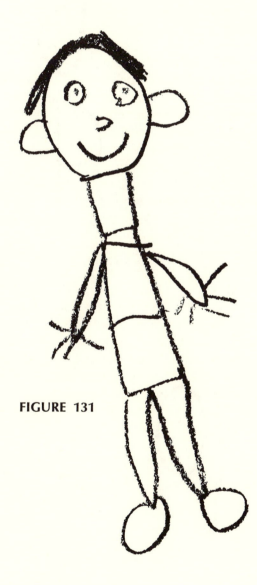

FIGURE 131

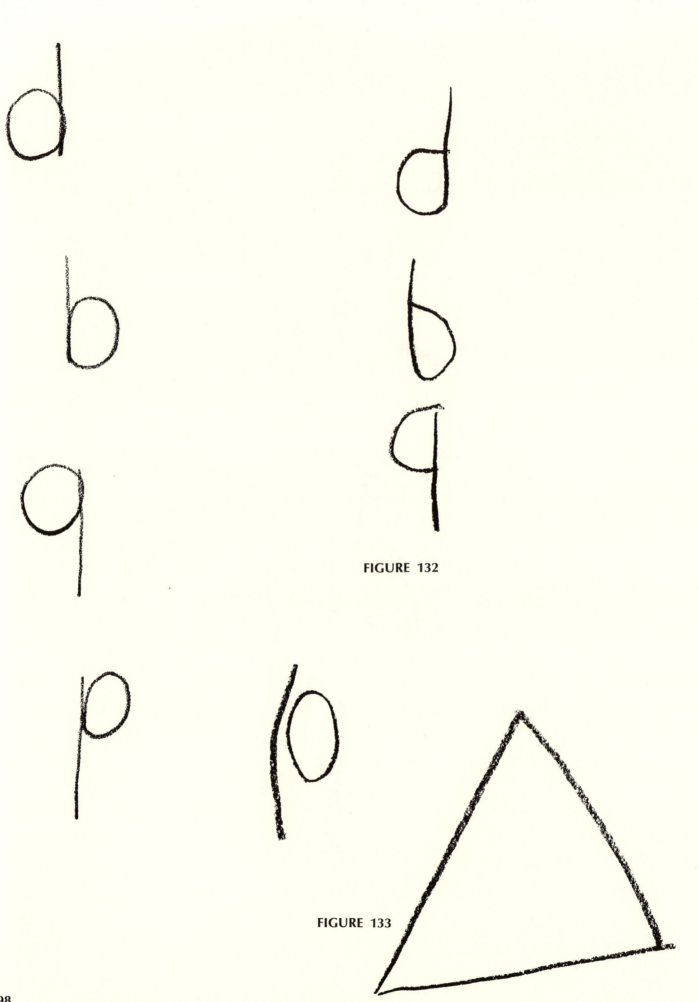

FIGURE 132

FIGURE 133

Phenylketonuria 2

Figures 134 through 137 show striking lack of progress in Draw-a-Person Test response. Treatment was begun early, at age one week, but the special low phenylalanine diet has not been adhered to consistently and the boy's blood levels of phenylalanine have been high. In response to the examiner's request that he draw a person, he has produced figures that are practically identical at ages 7, 9, 10 and 11 years.

The first figure, drawn at age 7, he called "a boy with a balloon." It expresses an intellectual maturity of 6 years 3 months. The second figure, which he said was "a girl holding a balloon, and she's walking," he drew at age 9. He has added hair to indicate the female. The third, drawn at age 10, is almost indistinguishable from the previous one. At age 11 he was again asked to draw a person. The result is a figure very similar to the earlier ones but larger, with very little added either qualitatively or quantitatively. The mouth is now two-dimensional, there are buttons on the dress, and the number of fingers on the left hand is correct. (Obsession or perseveration?)

Figures 138 and 139, copies of the Bender figures drawn at ages 10 and 11, show no improvement; if anything, they indicate regression in gestalt function. A poor result.

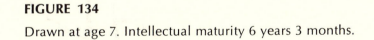

FIGURE 134

Drawn at age 7. Intellectual maturity 6 years 3 months.

FIGURE 135

Drawn at age 9 years 2 months, attending 3rd grade. General level of functioning is at the 7-year level with signs of perceptuo-motor impairment.

FIGURE 136

Drawn at age 10 years 2 months, repeating 3rd grade.

FIGURE 137

Drawn at age 10 years 10 months.

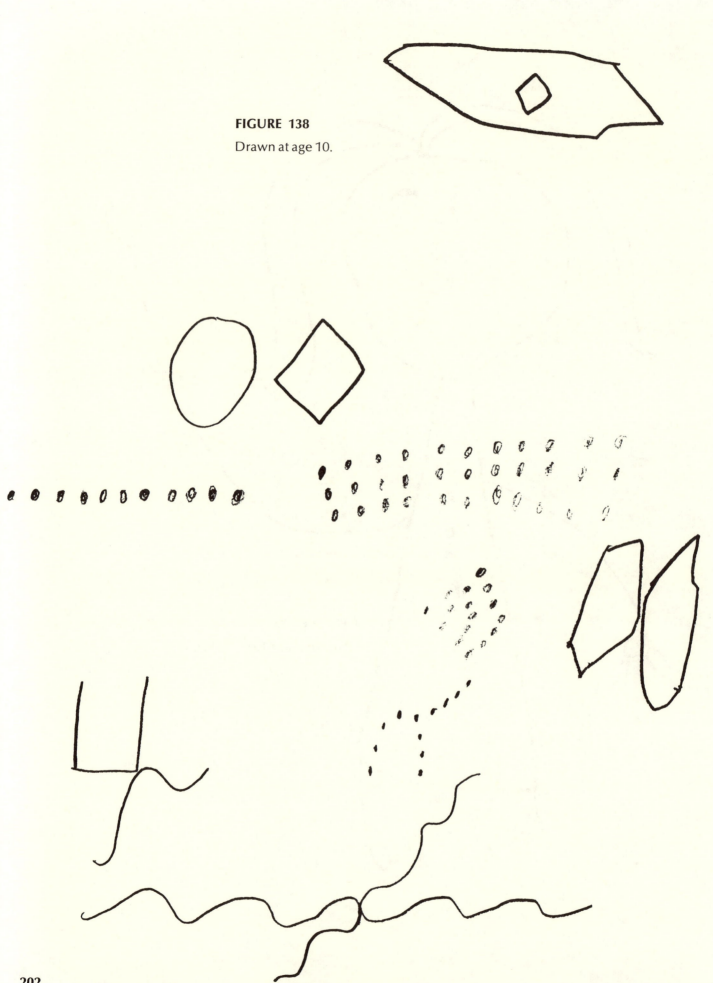

FIGURE 138
Drawn at age 10.

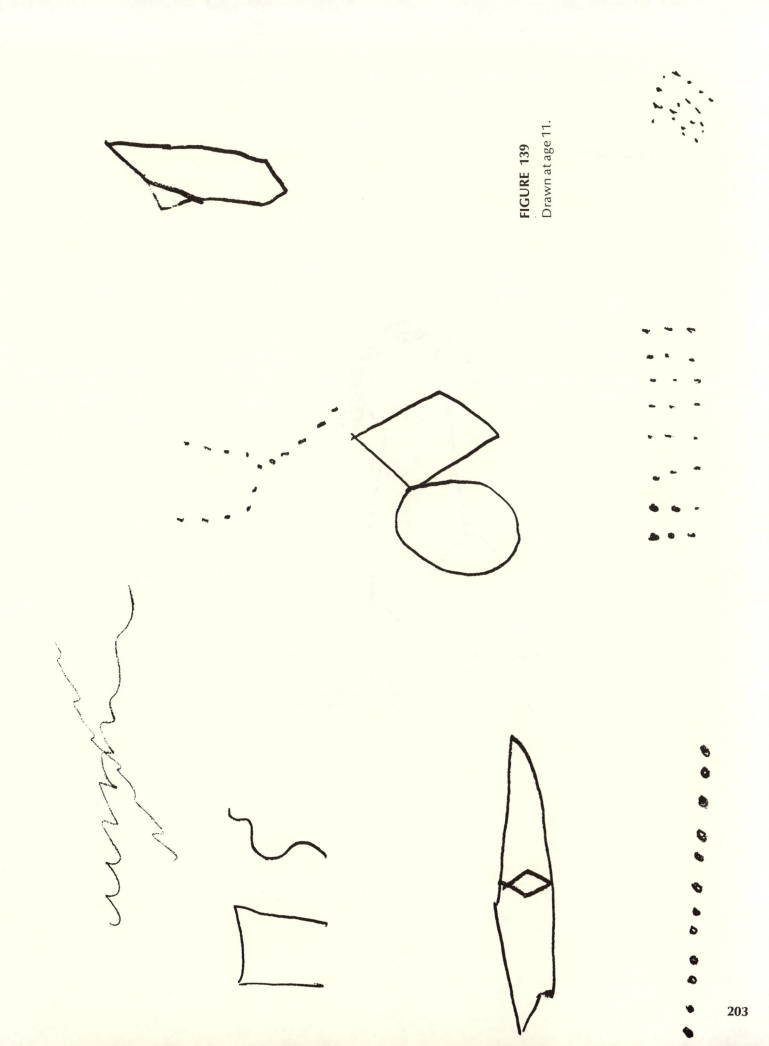

FIGURE 139
Drawn at age 11.

FIGURE 140

Treatment started at age 29 months was too late to be effective. The child is mentally retarded. The human figure drawn at chronological age 8 years 2 months expresses a mental age of 4 years 6 months.

FIGURE 141

Alerted by the above case, a subsequent child was diagnosed and treated promptly for the same recessive condition, phenylketonuria. At age 5 years 10 months, he is fully average in behavioral development, and his vocabulary is above average. The human figure drawing expresses an equivalent maturity. Good result.

Phenylketonuria 4

Figures 142 to 144 show a poor result. Treatment was initiated when the child was 2 years 9 months of age, discontinued at 10 years 6 months. Treatment was started too late to have any effect. The child is an educable retardate, passive and depressed. Although ineffectual as regards accelerating mental development, delayed treatment may still be helpful by reducing hyperactivity in some phenylketonuric children.

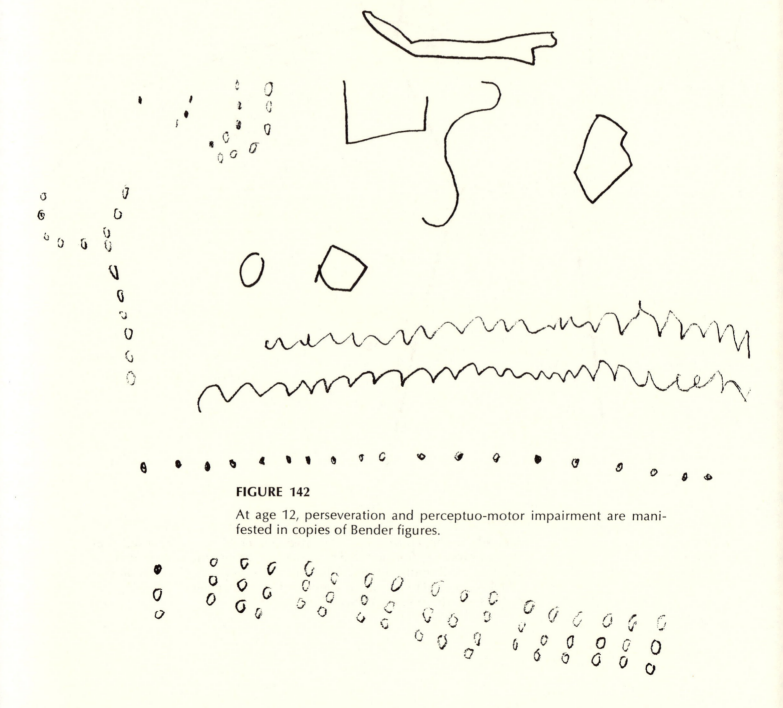

FIGURE 142

At age 12, perseveration and perceptuo-motor impairment are manifested in copies of Bender figures.

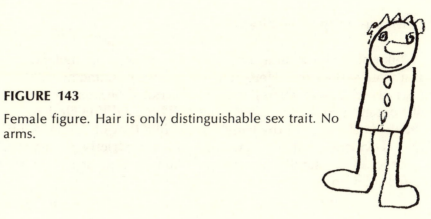

FIGURE 143

Female figure. Hair is only distinguishable sex trait. No arms.

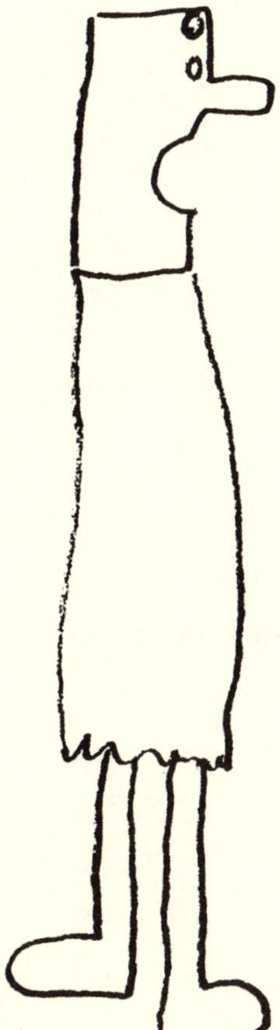

FIGURE 144

Male figure. Note mixed profile (two eyes, feet in frontal view) and absence of arms.

Maple syrup urine disease

Like phenylketonuria, this is an inborn error of metabolism but a more serious one. Here, not one but three amino acids (leucine, isoleucine, and valine) must be restricted because of genetically determined enzyme deficiencies. The condition derives its name from the odor of the baby's urine, like that of maple syrup. There is evidence that a special dietary regime, strictly carried out, can prevent the serious neurological damage that occurs in untreated children.

FIGURE 145

Drawn by a 9-year-old girl with retarded mental development due to maple syrup urine disease.

20

LEARNING DISABILITY
DUE TO EMOTIONAL PROBLEMS

When presented with a problem, one tends to search for a cause, usually a single cause that may account for the clinical manifestations.

Innumerable referrals are made in terms such as "we would like you to tell us whether he's mentally retarded or brain-damaged" . . . "brain-damaged or emotionally disturbed."

This tendency, to fit the child into a category that can be neatly computerized, loses sight of the fact that many mentally retarded children are also emotionally disturbed, and that many who are neurologically impaired may have serious personality problems. This is especially so when mental retardation or neurological deficit is not severe and the child is within striking distance of normal.

FIGURE 146

Figures 146 to 148 are drawn by a bright boy of 7 years 6 months who is doing poorly in second grade. Teacher complains that he dawdles and daydreams and engages in silly behavior. He reads and writes satisfactorily. There are no signs of perceptuo-motor impairment. At home, he is intensely jealous of his much-admired younger sister. Mother is the disciplinarian (he has drawn her with big arms and hands). He eats huge quantities of food. The child lacks confidence and motivation because of maternal disapproval. He often says, "I hate myself; put me in the garbage can." He prefers his dog to family members.

In the family drawing, he has isolated himself from the group and has portrayed himself with his dog.

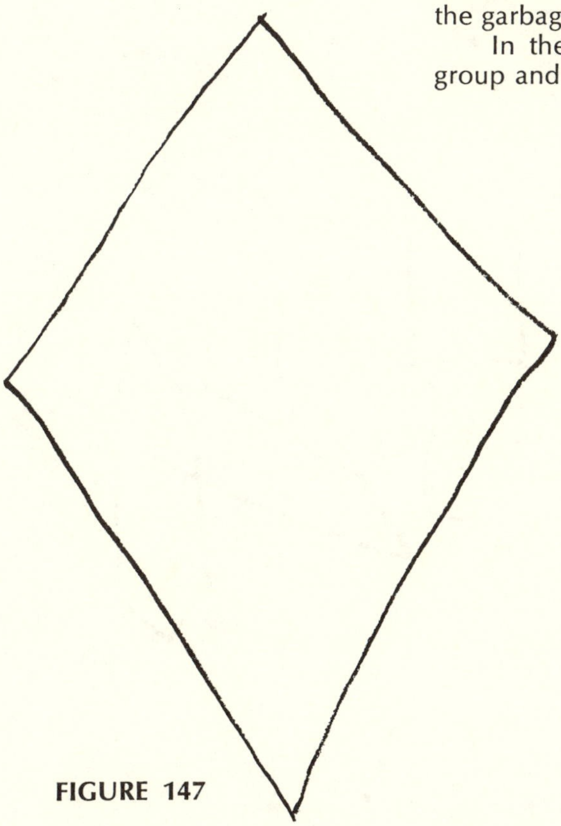

FIGURE 147

FIGURE 148

Note how single figure drawing is superior to human figures in the family drawing.

FIGURE 149

This 11-year-old boy is depressed, unmotivated. His school work is poor and he refuses to do homework. The emotional climate in the home is generally tense. The child is the object of much criticism. He feels inadequate and defeated. His copies of the test figures are indicative of normal visual-motor organization. There are no evidences of impaired gestalt function as in the earlier case of a 12½-year-old girl (**Figure 117**).

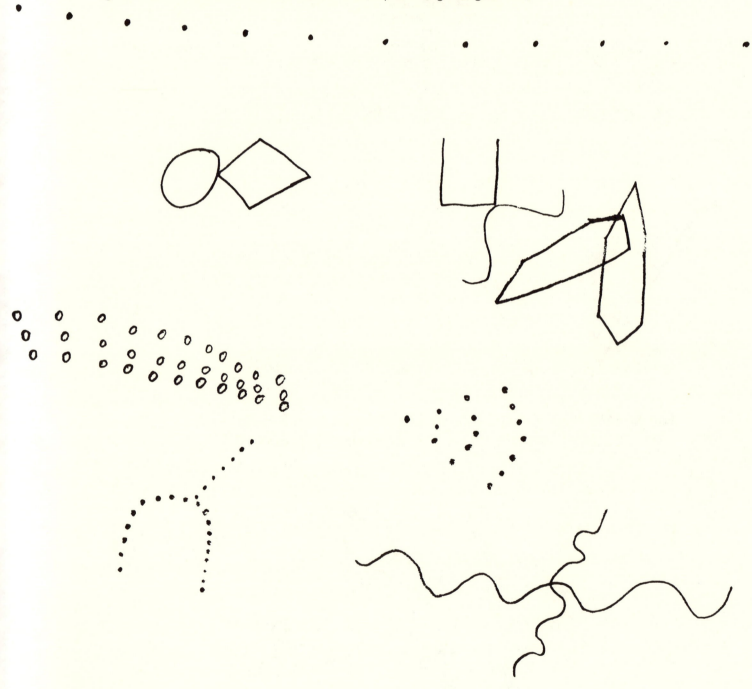

Epilogue

In this book, I have tried to show how helpful children's drawings can be to our understanding of behavior disorders. At intervals, enthusiasm has been tempered with the reminder that the drawings are but a part of a comprehensive evaluative process.

Among the topics discussed, I should like to single out the following for the reader's special consideration:

1. The concept of a cognitive/affective ratio, wherein more of one means less of the other. This see-saw effect is apparent in the difference between the human figure when drawn alone as compared with its rendition when it forms part of a family group. The superior quantitative as well as qualitative portrayal of the lone human figure is due, I believe, to the predominance of intellect when the child is asked simply to draw a person. But when the child is drawing the family group, the response tends to be influenced by affective elements. As a result, the figure in the family group may be less expressive of the child's intellectual maturity. As a practical point, intellectual maturity should not be evaluated from a human figure that forms part of a family group.

2. Human figure drawings and copies of simple geometric forms can be most helpful in the early diagnosis of perceptuo-motor difficulty and may be warning signals of future learning disorders, especially as they relate to the recognition and use of the symbols of the written word. Practical implication is the need for preschool perceptual training.

3. The vast majority of latency children draw their own sex first. A reversal of this tendency may indicate failure to adopt a sex role in conformity with biological sex. This may be due to excessive dominance by one parent or, as with institutionalized or fatherless children, absence of a male adult model. These situations call for the provision of opportunities to relate to adult parental figures of each sex.

4. Explicit portrayal of vulva or penis is rare in drawings by latency children. It often indicates maladjustment, castration fears, or more serious emotional disorder. It may simply express keen perception by a bright child. In any case, the fact warrants a second look.

5. The well adjusted child is less likely to draw a self-image. The figure drawn is usually an adult, a composite expressing the child's concept of a person. It is the anxiety-ridden child or the one

with a handicap that is more apt to turn his thoughts inward and draw himself.

6. Drawings are most helpful as diagnostic aids when they are personal expressions. In this category are those by young children who have not as yet been made to see things "correctly"; by emotionally disturbed persons whose perceptions are deviantly their own; and by the mentally retarded who are incapable of learning how to do it "right."

APPENDIX

Drawing situations: order of presentation
Validity and reliability of children's drawings

Drawing situations: order of presentation

In the administration of drawing tests, it is important to begin with spontaneous drawing. The examiner simply places paper and crayon or pencil before the child. Most children will begin to draw promptly; others may be told "make something"; some will say "I can't" and then proceed to comply after a little encouragement; very few will fail to respond. This last behavior is in itself revealing; it should be noted and related to other aspects of the child's behavior.

The specimen that the child produces spontaneously is the least structured, the least influenced from without, and therefore, often quite his own.

Once the spontaneous drawing has been obtained, the examiner will go on to the Draw-a-Person test with children over three. If the figure is a male, the child is asked to draw a female on another sheet of paper. The examiner notes which of the two was drawn first and whether sex differences are represented (usually more hair on the female head in the case of younger children; clothing and body contour as they grow older). This drawing is generally a valid expression of intelligence and as such correlates well with IQ tests such as the Stanford-Binet and the Wechsler. Disparity between the mental age derived from the Draw-a-Person test and the IQ tests is typical of emotional disorder or brain damage and has diagnostic significance.

The child is next asked to draw his family. This situation tends to mobilize the child's feelings vis-a-vis the most important people in his life. The result is often strikingly revealing of the child's self-image as related to other members of his family. Of particular significance are exaggerations of size: important persons are drawn larger, while less imposing persons are smaller. Rejected members of the family may be omitted; the child may even omit himself as a manifestation of feelings of rejection, not belonging, and inferiority. He will tend to place himself close to the loving parent and away from the punitive one. He may draw himself larger than a sibling who is older and physically larger. Preschool children will draw family members full-face and lined up in a row. Size, ordinal position, inclusion or omission are the principal revealing items.

When children are older and capable of depicting movement, the request will be "draw a picture of everyone in your family, including you, doing something." But this situation should follow and not replace the foregoing one because of the significance of omission of a family member and especially when the omitted one is the child himself. This kinetic-family-drawing has been used extensively by Burns and Kaufman and has proven revealing of the child's image of various family members and of the family pathology as he sees it. It is of value in school-age children and adolescents.

Copying should be relegated to the end of the series. These are structured situations and should not be given earlier as they may impair the freedom of expression that the examiner strives to maintain in the preceding situations. In this category of copying are the Bender figures and at the younger ages the request to copy circle, cross, triangle, square, and diamond. These tests are helpful in the detection of perceptuo-motor impairment, fine motor incoordination, and other manifestations of syndromes of cerebral dysfunctions.

Validity and reliability of children's drawings

The validity of human figure drawings as expressions of intellectual maturity has been demonstrated by numerous investigators who have reported statistically significant correlations with the Stanford-Binet and Wechsler Intelligence Scale for Children. The studies are reviewed by Harris (1963).

When the drawings are viewed as expressions of feelings, as projections of personality, the same degree of agreement has not been achieved. Here the subjective element in interpreting the drawings introduces a practically uncontrollable variable. Experience, insight, and intelligence play major roles and no two examiners possess these attributes to the same degree. Yet even in this diversity, there is evidence that personality traits expressed in the drawings correlate with those revealed by more extensive psychological and psychiatric interviews.

The question of reliability involves two aspects: the consistency among judges' ratings and consistency of the child with himself. Interjudge reliability has been convincingly demonstrated by several investigators, notably by Martin and Damrin. In a recent study, Ireton, Quast, and Gantcher have shown how a high degree of interjudge reliability was achieved by training nurses in the scoring of human figure drawings. This, of course, applies to ratings of intellectual maturity. The Goodenough-Harris Test was used.

The other aspect of reliability is one that continues to trouble some who are fascinated by children's drawings but yet wonder how to account for the differences between morning and afternoon productions or between those made on successive days. Apart from the fact that "backsliding" is a characteristic of all development and that progress must be evaluated over a long period, children's drawings show a remarkable degree of consistency. F. Goodenough reported a correlation of .937 between scores on two successive days. The study comprised 194 first-grade children. In an extensive study by Harris, the Draw-a-Person Test was given to four groups of kindergarten children on each of ten consecutive days. He found the variation to be "quite insignificant."

I have not found consistency to be a problem, provided the drawing being scored for intellectual maturity is a single human figure, not one in a family grouping. The reasons for this distinction have already been discussed. Another factor that may account for the consistency of my experience is the reduction of variables to a minimum. All my children drew in individual session. The setting was uniform, indeed it was the same room, the same procedure and, insofar as I could help myself, the same me saying "make a person." More variables are introduced in a group setting, more distractions.

Even so, there were children who drew one parent (generally the preferred one) more elaborately than the other. In that case, I scored the better of the two as more representative of the child's intelligence.

References

AMES, L. B., MÉTRAUX, R. W., and WALKER, R. N.: *Adolescent Rorschach Responses.* (revised ed.) New York, Brunner/Mazel. 1971

ANASTASI, A., and FOLEY, J. P. JR.: An analysis of spontaneous drawings by children in different cultures. *Jour. Appl. Psychol.* 20: 689-726, 1936.

ARISTOTLE: De Anima. Book III, 7. *The Works of Aristotle* (W. D. Ross, ed.). Oxford, Clarendon Press. Vol. III. 1931.

ARNHEIM, R.: *Art and Visual Perception.* Berkeley, Univ. of Calif. Press. 1965.

ARNHEIM, R.: *Visual Thinking.* Berkeley, Univ. of Calif. Press. 1969.

BADELL-RIBERA, A., SHULMAN, K., and PADDOCK, N.: The relationship of non-progressive hydrocephalus to intellectual functioning in children with spina bifida cystica. *Pediatrics.* 37:787-794.

BAKWIN, H., and BAKWIN, R. M.: *Clinical Management of Behavior Disorders in Children* (4th ed.). Philadelphia, Saunders. 1972.

BALLARD, P. B.: What London children like to draw. *J. Exper. Pedagogy.* 1:185-197, 1912.

BENCINI, P.: I Disegni dei Fanciulli. *Revista Pedagogia,* Vol. 1: 665-690. 1908.

BENDER, L.: The drawing of a man in chronic encephalitis in children. *J. Nerv. and Mental Dis.* 40:277-286. 1940.

BRITSCH, G.: *Theorie der bildenden Kunst.* Munich, F. Bruckmann. 1926.

BURNS, R. C., and KAUFMAN, S. H.: *Kinetic Family Drawings (K-F-D).* New York, Brunner/Mazel. 1970.

BURNS, R. C., and KAUFMAN, S. H.: *Actions, Styles and Symbols in Kinetic Family Drawings.* New York, Brunner/Mazel. 1972.

CHESS, S., KORN, S. J., and FERNANDEZ, P. B.: *Psychiatric Disorders of Children with Congenital Rubella.* New York, Brunner/Mazel. 1971.

CLAPARÈDE, E.: *Psychologie de l'Enfant et Pedagogie Expérimentale.* I. Le développment mental. Paris, Delachaux & Niestlé. 1946.

CRATTY, B. J., and SAMS, T. A.: *The Body Image of Blind Children.* Amer. Found. for the Blind. New York, July 1968.

CRITCHLEY, M.: *Developmental Dyslexia.* Springfield, C. C. Thomas. 1964.

DE BONO, E.: *The Dog Exercising Machine.* New York, Simon and Schuster. 1971.

DENNIS, W.: *Group Values Through Children's Drawings.* New York, J. Wiley. 1966.

DI LEO, J. H.: Early detection of developmental disorders, in *Learning Disabilities: its implications to a responsible society.* (D. Kronick, ed.) Chicago, Developmental Learning Materials. 1969.

DI LEO, J. H.: *Young Children and Their Drawings.* New York, Brunner/Mazel. 1970.

ENG, H.: *The Psychology of Children's Drawings* (2nd ed.). London, Routledge and Kegan Paul. 1954.

ERIKSON, E.: *Childhood and Society.* New York, W. W. Norton & Co. 1950.

FANTZ, R. L.: The predictive value of changes in visual preferences in early infancy, in *Exceptional Infant,* Vol. I. (J. Hellmuth, ed.) New York, Brunner/Mazel. 1967.

FATERSON, H. F., and WITKIN, H. A.: Longitudinal study of development of the body concept. *Developmental Psychol.* 2:429-438. 1970.

FISHLER, K.: Psychological assessment services, in *The Mentally Retarded Child and His Family.* (R. Koch and J. C. Dobson, eds.) New York, Brunner/Mazel. 1971.

FORGUS, R. H.: Perception, in *Behavioral Science in Pediatric Medicine* (N. B. Talbot, J. Kagan, and L. Eisenberg). Philadelphia, Saunders. 1971.

FREUD, A., and BURLINGHAM, D.: *Infants Without Families.* New York, Intern. Univ. Press. 1944.

FROSTIG, M., and HORNE, D.: *The Frostig Program for the Development of Visual Perception.* Chicago, Follett Pub. Co. 1964.

GESELL, A., and ILG, F. L.: *Infant and Child in the Culture of Today.* New York, Harper. 1943.

GESELL, A., ILG, F. L., and BULLIS, G. E.: *Vision: its development in infant and child.* New York, Hoeber. 1949.

GONDOR, L. H., and GONDOR, E. I.: Changing Times, in *Annual Progress in Child Psychiatry and Child Development* (S. Chess and A. Thomas, eds.). New York, Brunner/Mazel. 1970. pp. 288-299.

GOODENOUGH, F. L. *Measurement of Intelligence by Drawings.* New York, World Book Co. 1926.

GRAMS, M., and RINDER, W.: Signs of Homosexuality in Human Figure Drawings, in *Handbook of Projective Techniques* (B. I. Murstein, ed.). New York, Basic Books. 1965. pp. 683-685.

GREEN, M., and LEVITT, E. E.: Constriction of body image in children with congenital heart disease. *Pediatrics.* 29:438-442. Mar. 1962.

GRÖZINGER, W.: *Scribbling, Drawing, Painting.* New York, Praeger. 1955.

HARRIS, D. B.: *Children's Drawings as Measures of Intellectual Maturity.* New York, Harcourt, Brace and World. 1963.

HAUSER, S. T.: *Black and White Identity Formation.* New York, Wiley-Interscience. 1971.

IRETON, H., QUAST, W., and GANTCHER, P.: The Draw-a-Man Test as an index of developmental disorders in a pediatric outpatient population. *Child Psych. and Hum. Devel.* Vol. 2, No. 1. Fall 1971. 42-50.

JOHNSON, J. H.: Note on the validity of Machover's indicators of anxiety. *Perceptual & Motor Skills.* Vol. 33 (1). 126. 1971 (Aug.)

JOURDAIN, F.: L'Art et l'enfant. *Le Point. Revue Artistique et Litteraire.* Mulhouse, France. Juillet 1953. pp. 9-19.

JUNG, C. G.: *Analytical Psychology. Its Theory and Practice.* London, Routledge and Kegan Paul. 1968.

KATZAROFF, M. D.: Qu'est-ce que les enfants dessinent? *Arch. de Psychol.* 9:125-233. 1909-1910.

KERSCHENSTEINER, D. G.: *Die Entwickelung der zeichnerischen Begabung.* Munich, Gerber. 1905.

KOPPITZ, E. M.: *Psychological Evaluation of Children's Human Figure Drawings.* New York, Grune & Stratton. 1968.

KRAMER, E.: *Art as Therapy with Children.* New York, Schocken Books. 1971.

LAMPRECHT, K.: See Levinstein, *Anhang.*

LEVINSTEIN, S.: *Kinderzeichnungen bis zum 14 Lebensjahr.* Leipzig, R. Voigtlander Verlag. 1905. *Anhang* by LAMPRECHT, K.

LEWIS, H. P. (ed): *Child Art: The Beginnings of Self-Affirmation.* Berkeley, Calif. Diablo Press. 1973.

LIDZ, T.: The family as the developmental setting, in *The Child and His Family* (E. J. Anthony and C. Koupernik, eds.). New York, Wiley-Interscience. 1970. p. 20.

LINDSAY, Z.: *Art and the Handicapped Child.* New York, Van Nostrand Reinhold, 1972.

LISENCO, YASHA: *Art Not by Eye.* New York. Amer. Found. for the Blind. 1972.

LOWENFELD, V., and BRITTAIN, W. L.: *Creative and Mental Growth* (4th ed.). New York, Macmillan. 1964.

LUKENS, H.: A study of children's drawings in the early years. *Pedagogical Seminary.* 4:79-110.

LUQUET, G. H.: *Les Dessins d'un Enfant: etude psychologique. Librairie Felix Alcan. Paris.* 1913.

LYDDIATT, E. M.: *Spontaneous Painting and Modelling.* London, Constable. 1970.

MACHOVER, K.: *Personality Projection in the Drawing of the Human Figure.* Springfield, C. C. Thomas. 1949.

MACHOVER, K.: Human figure drawing of children. *J. Proj. Tech.* 17:53-92. 1953.

MARTIN, W. E., and DAMRIN, D. E.: An analysis of the reliability and factorial composition of ratings of children's drawings. *Child Devel.* 22:134-144. June 1951.

MILLER, E., and SETHI, L.: The effect of hydrocephalus on perception. *Devel. Med. and Child Neurol.* 1971. 13. Supp. 25.

MÜHLE, G.: *Entwicklungspsychologie des zeichnerischen Gestaltens.* München, Johann Ambrosius Barth. 1955.

NATHAN, S., and PISULA, D.: Adolescent obesity. *J. Amer. Acad. Child Psychiat.* 9:726-730. Oct. 1970.

NATIONAL CENTER FOR HEALTH STATISTICS: Intellectual Maturity of Children as Measured by the Goodenough-Harris Drawing Test. *Vital and Health Statistics.* PHS Pub. No. 1000—Series 11—No. 105. Public Health Service. Washington. U.S. Govt Printing Office, Dec. 1970.

NORRIS, M., SPAULDING, P. J., and BRODIE, F. H.: *Blindness in Children.* Chicago, Univ. of Chicago Press. 1957.

PALMER, J. O.: *The Psychological Assessment of Children.* New York, J. Wiley. 1970.

PARTRIDGE, L.: Children's drawings of men and women. *Studies in Education* by E. Barnes, 2:163-179. 1902.

PENFIELD, W., and RASMUSSEN, T.: *The Cerebral Cortex of Man.* New York, Macmillan. 1952.

PIAGET, J.: *The Language and Thought of the Child.* Cleveland, Meridian Books-World Publ. Co. 1966.

PIAGET, J., and INHELDER, B.: *Mental Imagery in the Child.* New York, Basic Books. 1971.

PIOTROWSKA, I., and SOBESKI M.: The Primitive. *J. Aesthetics and Art Criticism.* Winter 1941-1942. pp. 12-20.

PORTER, J. D. R.: *Black Child, White Child.* Cambridge, Harvard Univ. Press. 1971.

PRUDHOMMEAU, M.: *Le Dessin de l'Enfant.* Paris, Presses Universitaires de France. 1947.

READ, H.: *Art and Society.* Schocken Books. New York. 1966.

RICCI, C.: *L'Arte dei Bambini.* Bologna, Zanichelli editore. 1887.

ROUMA, G.: *El Lenguaje Gráfico del Niño* (trans. by De Someillán, A.). Havana, Gutierrez y Comp. 1919.

SCHILDER, P.: *The Image and Appearance of the Human Body.* New York, Intern. Univ. Press. 1950.

SCHILDER, P.: *Contributions to Developmental Neuropsychiatry* (L. Bender, ed.). New York, Intern. Univ. Press. 1964.

SCHILDKROUT, M. S., SHENKER, I. R., and SONNENBLICK, M.: *Human Figure Drawings in Adolescence.* New York, Brunner/Mazel. 1972.

SPEARING, H. G.: *The Childhood of Art.* New York, H. Holt. 1912.

STERN, W.: *Psychology of Early Childhood* (trans. by A. Barwell). New York, H. Holt. 1924.

STITES, R. B.: *The Sublimations of Leonardo da Vinci*. Washington, D.C., Smithsonian Instit. Press. 1970.

SULLY, J.: *Studies of Childhood*. London, Longmans, Green. 1895.

SUNDBERG, N. D.: The Practice of Psychological Testing in Clinical Services in the United States, in *The Clinical Psychologist* (B. Lubin and E. E. Levitt, eds.). Chicago, Aldine Publ. Co. 1967. pp. 155-162.

TAYLOR, I. A.: The Nature of the Creative Process, in *Creativity—an examination of the creative process* (P. Smith, ed.). New York, Hastings House. 1959.

TOKER, E.: Psychiatric aspects of cardiac surgery in a child. *J. Amer. Acad. Child Psychiat.* 10:176-182. Jan. 1971.

TREVOR-ROPER, P.: *The World Through Blunted Sight*. Indianapolis, Bobbs-Merrill. 1970.

ULRICH, S.: *Elizabeth*. Ann Arbor, Univ. of Michigan Press. 1972.

U.S. DEPT. OF HEALTH, EDUCATION, AND WELFARE. NINDS Monograph No. 9, *Central Processing Dysfunctions in Children: a review of research.* 1969.

VANE, J. R., and EISEN, V. W.: The Goodenough Draw-a-Man Test and signs of maladjustment in kindergarten children, in *Handbook of Projective Techniques* (B. I. Murstein, ed.). New York, Basic Books. 1965. pp. 685-691.

WINNICOTT, D. W.: *Therapeutic Consultations in Child Psychiatry*. New York, Basic Books. 1971.

WOLFF, W.: *The Personality of the Preschool Child*. New York, Grune & Stratton. 1946.

WYSOCKI, B. A., and WYSOCKI, A. C.: The body-image of normal and retarded children. *Journ. Clin. Psychol.* Vol. 29, No. 1. 1973 (Jan.).

Index of names

Index of subjects

houses, 10
human figure, 8, 20, 21, 23, 26, 27, 30-33, 144-146, 172, 176, 216, passim
hydrocephalus, 150
hyperactivity, 166, 206

identity, 79
imagery, 27, 128, 130, 156
impaired hearing, 134-138
impaired vision, 132-134
individuality, 23
inferiority feelings, 157, 216
insecurity, 36, 37, 42, 48
institution children, 4, 5, 57, 66, 96, 213
intellectual maturity, 18, 26, 27, 217
intellectual realism, 8, 27, 113
intelligence, 18, 30, 32, 106, 123, 144-146, 164, 172, 176, 216, 218
interaction, 105, 117
internal model, 8, 27
isolation, 105, 117
Italian language, 182

Japanese children, 117, 182
jealousy, 109, 119, 211

kinetic family drawings, 105, 117-119, 217
kinesthetic drawing, 4, 6
Kopffüssler, 14, 26
"knowing" child, 121-124

language, phonetic, 182
language, pictographic, 182
latency children, 54, 79, 105, 122, 213
lateral dominance, 182
laterality, 182
learning disabilities, 145, 162-180, 213
legs, 14, 22, 26

maple syrup urine disease, 208
marriage, 51, 52
masculinity, 57, 62, 64
masturbation, 51
mental health, 48
mental retardation, body image in, 190-210
mental retardation, learning disability due to, 190-208, 214
minimal brain dysfunction, 32, 165-180
mixed profile, 26, 34, 207
modeling, 182
mother, 15, 115, 130
mothering, 23
motivation, 182
motor disability, 144
mouth, absence of, 38, 65, 135, 136, 156
movement, 4, 23, 26, 27, 57, 132, 144
mutism, 87

National Center for Health Statistics, 27, 190
neurologically impaired, 30-33, 139, 210
nose, 26

obesity, 156, 157
omission of body parts, 15, 34, 38-42, 190, 207
omission of family member, 108, 216
omission of self, 109, 110, 216
operational thought, 16
organic brain syndrome, 144, 145

perception, 4, 20, 22, 144, 150, 164
perceptual training, 165, 213, 182
perceptuo-motor, 30, 33, 145-150, 165, 166, 213, 217
peripheral hearing loss, 134
perseveration, 33, 145, 177-180, 199, 206
personality, 18, 30, 48, 68, 130, 134
phenylketonuria, 196-207
position, relative, 109, 112, 216
postcentral gyrus, 130
precentral gyrus, 130
prehistoric man, 4
preoperational thought, 164
projective technique, 31, 100, 105, 106
pseudohermaphrodite, 65
psychobiological unity, ix

racial differences in drawings, 21, 22
realism, inner, 8
realism, intellectual versus visual, 8, 26, 113
realism, visual, ix, 8, 27, 34
rejection, 105, 216
relative size, 113
representational drawing, 4, 8, 9
reproduction, interest in, 51, 122
retina, 128, 133
reversals, 186
Rh incompatibility, 177
rigid, robot-like figure, 36, 76, 77
role, sex, 36, 42, 57
Rorschach, 30, 79, 156
rubella, congenital, 134

scatter of body parts, 36, 68, 69
schizophrenic children, 91
scribbling, 26, 34
security, 36, 37, 42
seduction, 54
segregation, 22
Self, concept of, 20
self-esteem, 106, 182
self image, 20, 106, 213, 216
sensation, 9
sense and motion, 130
sensory impairment, 23
sex drawn first, 216
sex, explicit expression of, 36, 54, 56, 213
sex, symbolic expression of, 54, 57
sex role, 36, 42, 57-65, 117, 213
shading as expression of anxiety, 36, 79-81
similarity, 113
size, significance of, 22, 113, 216
small figures, 22, 36, 115, 156, 157
square, copy of, 217